The Structure of Wages in Latin American Manufacturing Industries

The Structure of Wages in Latin American Manufacturing Industries

Jorge Salazar-Carrillo

with Juan J. Buttari, Francisco J. Ortega,
and Adalberto García Rocha

A Florida International University Book
University Presses of Florida
Miami

Original Spanish language edition *(Estructura de los salarios industriales en América Latina)* © 1979 Ediciones S.I.A.P., Buenos Aires, Argentina. Published in the Programa de Estudios Conjuntos sobre Integración Económica Latinoamericana (ECIEL).

Library of Congress Cataloging in Publication Data

Salazar-Carrillo, Jorge.
  The structure of wages in Latin American manufacturing industries.

  "A Florida International University book."
  Bibliography: p.
  Includes index.
  1. Wages—Latin America.   I. Buttari, Juan J.,
joint author.   II. Title.
HD4980.5.S24   331.2′87′098   80-25072
ISBN 0-8130-0696-1

University Presses of Florida is the central agency for scholarly publishing of the State of Florida's university system. Its offices are located at 15 NW 15th Street, Gainesville, FL 32603. Works published by University Presses of Florida are evaluated and selected by the faculty editorial committees of Florida's nine public universities: Florida A&M University (Tallahassee), Florida Atlantic University (Boca Raton), Florida International University (Miami), Florida State University (Tallahassee), University of Central Florida (Orlando), University of Florida (Gainesville), University of North Florida (Jacksonville), University of South Florida (Tampa), University of West Florida (Pensacola).

Printed in the United States.

Contents

List of figures and tables

Figures

Tables

Chapter 1. Introduction

Wage differentials reflecting diverse skills and productivity components, or resulting from such factors as disequilibria, market imperfections, and transfer costs, define the wage structure of a particular country or region. Accordingly, the wage structure constitutes a "formal way of describing the distribution of wages in any given situation."[1]

The measurement and study of wage differentials is essential for an understanding of labor market performance at local, national, or regional levels. The importance of wage differentials was formally recognized at least two centuries ago and has led contemporary writers to refer to them as among the more interesting problems for research in labor economics in developing countries.[2] The significance attributed to this topic can hardly be exaggerated when account is taken of the important role that wage differentials play in determining labor mobility and migration: for it is through the wage structure that the labor market tends to allocate labor to situations where its productivity and wages are higher; changes in wage differentials may have important implications for poverty and for income distribution. Moreover, through their impact on production costs, wage differentials act as partial determinants of production and technological patterns. Consequently, they have important potential effects on production and trade possibilities.

In spite of its importance, systematic study of wage differentials in Latin America is of relatively recent origin and has been hampered by the lack of adequate data. Needless to say, the difficulties are compounded when measuring and examining the Inter-American structure of wages. In such circumstances, this study is a pioneering endeavor.[3]

1. International Labour Office, "Changing Wage Structure: An International Review," *International Labour Review* 73 (January–June 1956), p. 275.

2. See Adam Smith's chapter 10, book I, of *The Wealth of Nations* (Modern Library edition, 1937) and Lloyd C. Reynolds, *Relative Earnings and Manpower Allocation in Developing Economies,* Yale University Economic Growth Center Paper 134 (New Haven, Conn.: 1969).

3. For an earlier attempt with a different focus see John R. Eriksson, "Wage Structures and Economic Development in Selected Latin American Countries, A Comparative Analysis" (Ph.D. diss., University of California, Berkeley, 1966).

1

Purpose

Table 1-1 lists most of the principal wage differentials likely to be of importance in developing countries. This table suggests that many of the differentials are interrelated and that their effects may be compounding.

The main purpose of this study is to determine and analyze the structure of manufacturing wages in those developing countries forming the Latin American Free Trade Association (LAFTA): Argentina, Bolivia, Brazil, Chile, Colombia, Ecuador, Mexico, Paraguay, Peru, Uruguay, and Venezuela. It will concentrate on certain kinds of wage differentials, namely, intercountry wage differences within the LAFTA region, interindustry and intraindustry wage dispersion within each country, and differences in com-

Table 1-1. Principal types of wage differentials

Primary classification	Subclassification
Interoccupational	1. White collar / blue collar 2. Skilled / unskilled 3. Professional / nonprofessional
Interfirm	1. By size 2. By productivity
Interindustry	1. By sector (e.g., agriculture, industry, services, etc.) 2. By nature of product (e.g., durable / nondurable) 3. By product line (e.g., textiles, foodstuffs, etc.)
Geographical	1. Interregional 2. Intercity 3. Urban / rural
Unionization	1. By firm 2. By industry 3. By region
Demographical characteristics	1. By sex 2. By race 3. By age 4. By education

pensation according to occupational characteristics. Besides providing necessary information for the analysis of potential trade and migration patterns within Latin America, the present study attempts to furnish an empirical frame of reference for future in-depth studies of labor markets in the region.

The economic literature is full of examples in which wage differentials are measured according to one particular variable or another. However, as noted previously, in real life the various effects these variables have on wages are bound together. Under such conditions it is impossible to determine the wage differential caused by one factor unless the impact of the others is considered.

Until very recently it was customary to measure wage differentials in a "gross" fashion, with no attempt at extricating the influence of other variables not pertinent to the measurement. This study goes further, using the concept of "net" differentials. These are defined as wage differentials that measure the effect of a particular variable on wages after accounting for the impact on wages of other relevant factors.

Scope

In order to make the study feasible, its scope had to be limited in several respects. First, research was restricted to the manufacturing sector. Nine representative industries were selected in turn within manufacturing, and emphasis was given to three of them—metallurgy, textiles, and pharmaceuticals.

Second, special attention was given to the modern sector within the industries selected. The largest and most efficient firms were surveyed, especially those that were exporting or were considered potential exporters.

Third, not all occupations were covered. On the average, twenty positions per firm were surveyed, with special consideration given to twelve key positions, selected to represent the majority of clerical and plant positions in manufacturing. The concept of job clusters developed by Dunlop was used in selecting these positions in terms of their representativeness.[4]

The measurement of wage differentials was based on two kinds of wage concepts: take-home pay and labor cost. In both, special attention was given to a comparable and comprehensive treatment of fringe benefits. The wage surveys also collected information on the levels of education, experience, and degree of responsibility required to perform satisfactorily in the administrative and plant positions covered. Data on these variables are crucial in order to ensure that the various wage differentials considered in the

4. John T. Dunlop, "The Task of Contemporary Wage Theory," in *The Theory of Wage Determination*, ed. John T. Dunlop (New York: Macmillan, 1957), pp. 3–27.

study are not distored by the effect of divergent skill requirements across countries, across industries, etc. Thus, it was possible to account for the effects of these variables and to consider only net wage differentials.[5]

Relevance of the study

Latin American countries have been undergoing a formal process of economic integration since the middle fifties.[6] As their economies draw closer, comparisons of wage levels and structures among these countries become necessary. Labor is the largest component of factor costs and therefore, as indicated, is important in the study of potential trade patterns within the area. Greater freedom of movement within the region is also expected to bring about increased labor migration, which would probably ultimately respond to pay differentials in real terms.

Crude estimates of LAFTA wage levels can be found.[7] Information on the structure of wages, however, is almost nonexistent. Because labor is not homogeneous, such information is essential for precise wage analysis.[8]

Countries may have wage advantages only for certain skill levels, industries, etc.; a comparative analysis of wage structures would provide such information. Moreover, trade is ultimately determined by relative costs. Even though the wages of a particular country may average high in absolute terms, certain labor services may be low priced relative to others. Thus goods produced by the intensive use of this kind of labor may have favorable export prospects.

Research on the structure of wages in LAFTA countries is also relevant for development policy and planning. Viewed as an independent variable influencing economic development, the role of the wage structure is mainly tied to the performance of the labor market as a mechanism for allocating resources. If the wage structure does not perform adequately as an alloca-

5. Other pertinent data were also gathered. These ranged from the size of the firm to the cities in which the firms were located, from the number of employees per occupation to the timing of labor contracts. These were helpful in attaining a more precise measurement of the wage differences investigated in this study, as well as in providing complementary information for the analysis.

6. For further reference see Joseph Grunwald, Miguel Wionczek, and Martin Carnoy, *Latin American Economic Integration and United States Policy* (Washington, D.C.: Brookings Institution, 1972).

7. See International Labor Office, *Yearbook of Labor Statistics,* Geneva, various years; Organization of American States, *America en Cifras,* Washington, D.C., various years; Joseph Ramos, *Labor and Development in Latin America* (New York: Columbia University Press, 1970).

8. Wages might be lower in certain countries because the levels of education and experience required to perform a particular job are also lower. In this case, the low wages may be neutralized by a lower intrinsic productivity of labor.

tive device, economic inefficiency and unemployment would result, which in turn would affect adversely the growth of production and incomes. Given the gap in knowledge relating to the performance of individual labor markets, exhaustive explanations of intercountry differentials are not possible at this time. Nevertheless, work along the lines followed in this study is useful for testing the factual consistency of existing hypotheses on labor market dynamics and for suggesting new ones.

Given the role of wage differentials in the efficient allocation of resources, it has been hotly debated, for example, whether these should be wide or narrow, and how different they should be from those in developed countries.[9] Obviously, this question also impinges on the distribution of income, of which wage differentials are an important determinant. Once the relevance of wage structure for development policy is understood, it is then pertinent to consider the ways in which it can be manipulated, and how certain variables could affect it. The analysis and results presented here, it is hoped, will stimulate further research on these points.

Plan of the book

The study is divided into three parts. This introductory part presents, in chapters 2 and 3, the conceptual and methodological framework followed in the study and a description of the survey data and methods used. The concept of "net" wage differentials is developed and details on the kinds of data gathered are provided.

In the second part of the book the wage structures of LAFTA countries are examined comparatively. In each country, wages are cross-classified according to industry, size of firm, worker's occupation or position, and various qualitative factors (education, etc.). Intercountry wage differentials are then estimated after the effects of the variables just indicated have been eliminated, which amounts to the estimation of these differentials in "net" terms.

The third part and an appendix contain the results of individual country studies, which investigate various aspects of the wage structure in these particular countries, focusing on interindustry wage spread and on occupational wage differentials. Finally, a concluding chapter summarizes the most salient results, compares the conclusions reached in the various country studies, and offers some generalizations and policy implications.

9. On these points see H. Zoeteweij, "Wage Policy and Economic Devlopment," in International Institute for Labour Studies, *Lectures on Labour and Economic Development* (Geneva: International Labor Office, 1963) and Walter Galenson, ed., *Labor in Developing Economies* (Berkeley: University of California Press, 1963).

Chapter 2. The basic conceptual and methodological framework

When examining quantitative results in later chapters, plausible explanations relying on fundamental concepts of marginal productivity wage theory and institutional factors will be frequently offered. Given the pioneering character of this study, the nature of the analytical comments should be made clear early in the work. These comments will be essentially interpretive and will often reflect educated conjecture relating to variables influencing the empirical findings. The lack of in-depth studies on specific labor markets (referred to in the previous chapter) makes a different approach not yet feasible.

In interpreting the quantitative results, three basic assumptions of marginal productivity theory will be employed: the rationality of employers and workers; the employer's desire to maximize net returns from factor inputs; and employees' aspiration to maximize the utility derived from their labor services. As is well known, from these assumptions the main principles of the theory are derived: (1) an employer will hire an extra unit of labor as long as the revenue from its marginal product is greater than or equal to its marginal cost; (2) an employee will provide additional labor services as long as the wage rate is greater than or equal to the marginal rate of substitution of income for leisure;[1] (3) equilibrium will be reached when marginal revenue produced is equal to marginal labor cost and when the wage rate is equal to the income-leisure marginal substitution rate.

Likewise applied will be the knowledge that under the Robinson-Chamberlain conditions varying product and factor market combinations will produce diverse wage rates and employment levels. Once a framework of different combinations of product and factor market situations is established and different types of labor factors are specified, the presence of wage differentials follows by implication, even under equilibrium conditions.[2]

1. The marginal rate of substitution is the number of units of a good a person is willing to give up to obtain an additional unit of another good.
2. See Lloyd Reynolds, "Wage Differences in Local Labor Markets," *American Economic*

Nevertheless, although the view taken in this book is that the above mentioned concepts and the theoretical models built on them are essential in any study of wage determination, they do not suffice. Account has to be taken of the influence of institutional factors as well as of the existence of compensatory wage differentials (i.e., differentials reflecting voluntary decisions by the workers due to the influence of nonmoney variables). Also important in analyzing wage differentials is the fact that labor is non-homogeneous—which gives rise to a spectrum of marginal productivities and workers' utility maps.

Collective bargaining and union power, government employment, and wage and social legislation, among other institutional factors, may exert substantial influence. The effect of each of these factors may produce a wage structure differing from the one that would prevail under pure marginal productivity theory conditions. In an overall context, a higher degree of labor and product market imperfections seems to exist in developing countries, although not all a priori reasoning points in this direction (for example, in developing countries union pressures generally seem to be weaker than in developed economies). In later chapters references will be made to the likely outcomes of various institutional factors.[3]

Other conceptual constructs such as Dunlop's job clusters and wage contours are useful complements to conventional marginal productivity theory (which intertwines well with the methodological approach followed in the study) and will be occasionally referred to later on.[4] A job cluster is "a stable group of job classifications or work assignments . . . which are linked together by (1) technology, (2) the administrative organization of the production process . . . , or (3) social custom—[so] that they have common wage-making characteristics."[5] A wage contour is "a stable group of wage-determining units . . . linked together by (1) similarity of product markets, (2) resort to similar sources for a labor force, or (3) common labor-market organization . . . [so] that they have common wage-making characteristics."[6] These concepts enable this study to focus on a relatively

Review 36 (1946), pp. 336–75; and Belton M. Fleisher, *Labor Economics: Theory and Evidence* (Englewood Cliffs, N.J.: Prentice Hall, 1970) for elaborate treatments of these points.

3. For discussion of the way these factors might affect wage determination see Fleisher, *Labor Economics,* and Peter Gregory, "The Impact of Institutional Factors on Urban Labor Markets" (paper presented at the 1975 International Bank for Reconstruction and Development Workshop on Urban Poverty).

4. John T. Dunlop, "The Task of Contemporary Wage Theory," in *New Concepts in Wage Determination,* ed. George Taylor and Frank Pierson (New York: McGraw Hill, 1957).

5. Ibid., p. 129.

6. Ibid., p. 131. Both concepts suggested by Dunlop can be well fitted within marginal productivity analysis. For an enlightening exposition see E. E. Liebhafsky, "A New Concept

few occupations and units and to analyze the determinants of those wages in depth.

In examining intercountry wage differentials use will be made of the fact that under conditions of complete international labor mobility, perfect information, purely economically motivated individuals, and competitive labor markets in the countries involved, intercountry wage differentials for homogeneous labor units should correspond solely to migration costs.

Summing up, a positive correlation between skills, productivity, and wages is hypothesized. Accordingly, a starting point for analysis is the belief that, although imperfectly, wage differentials reflect productivity differentials. Dissimilarities between the structure of both sets of differentials are interpreted as reflecting the combined effect of adjustment lags, inadequate information, transfer costs, physical barriers to mobility, and institutional factors.

From what has already been indicated, it follows that to a considerable degree wage differentials may reflect differences in the quality of labor arising from such variables as innate ability, formal and informal training, and health. These qualities may be thought of as forming diverse skill and productivity components commanding different wages at the firm and industry levels. Moreover, diversity in occupational job content as well as in factors specific to firms, industries, and countries also has an impact upon wage differences. Thus, when measuring wage differentials one should control for the effect of these variables. A first step is adjusting for the effects of skills and of job contents.

This problem could be partially surmounted by defining a uniform set of tasks for the different occupations considered in each country or industry. This is not, however, enough, as such definitions would have to be unrealistically precise in order to remove completely the influence of labor heterogeneity.[7] A more adequate approach would be to use regression techniques in conjunction with a relatively new interpretation of demand theory known as the hedonic technique.[8]

---

in Wage Determination: Disguised Productivity Analysis," *Southern Economic Journal* 26 (October 1959), pp. 141–46.

7. The tasks would have to be very minutely defined. In that case, it would be practically impossible to find a sufficient number of comparable sets of uniform tasks in different industries or countries. Conversely, to make comparison possible, the uniform set of tasks would have to be defined too generally.

8. See Kelvin Lancaster, *Consumer Demand: A New Approach* (New York: Columbia University Press, 1971). The term *hedonic*, it should be made clear, does not imply any connection with the philosophical doctrine which sees pleasure as the principal good.

The hedonic technique applied to wage comparisons

The hedonic approach is a method that facilitates the comparison of different kinds of prices (wages included) by ensuring that the quality to which they refer is as homogeneous as possible. This is done by decomposing each good or service (including labor services) into the characteristics or components that define it (horsepower, durability, and compactness in cars, for example). Through the use of regression, implicit prices for such characteristics in different markets can be estimated. Once these are known, it is possible to estimate the price of any good, service, or factor of production for a uniform combination of characteristics or components in various markets.[9]

The implicit price for each characteristic is estimated through multiple regression methods in which the total price for the specific good or service is the dependent variable and certain of its various characteristics are the independent variables. Usually a reasonably large number of observations on the price of the good or service in question and corresponding information on its characteristics, in physical terms, are required for the estimation of a regression equation. The slope coefficients constitute the implicit prices for the respective characteristics.

An illustration may be useful. Consider the case of typists. Those performing a particular function can be categorized by a certain number of qualitative elements: so many years of training or education, so much experience, and the like. Let us concentrate on just the education or training variable. For two different kinds of typing services, an employer may require a high school diploma for one and a high school diploma plus a year of training in a secretarial school for the other, and he may pay a higher salary for the better trained typist. At the same time, considering the cost of an extra year of training, the second typist would normally be willing to work only at higher wages.

In this example, the only difference between the two jobs is the one year of specialized training required for the second kind of typist. Thus, the pay difference between them can be attributed to this factor. In general, if a regression is run using the wages of typists as the dependent variable and their years of education as the independent variable, the slope coefficient measures the price that would be paid for an additional year of education. The implicit prices of these qualitative characteristics would be expected to

9. For further information on the hedonic approach see Zvi Griliches, "Introduction: Hedonic Price Indexes Revisited," in *Price Indexes and Quality Changes,* ed. Zvi Griliches (Cambridge, Mass.: Harvard University Press, 1971).

diverge among markets, depending on their degree of isolation. Thus, they probably would differ more from country to country and less among the various labor markets in a particular country.[10]

A graphical analysis

The problems of heterogeneity of labor in comparing wages across countries or industries, and the ways in which they are solved by the hedonic approach, can be depicted by simple diagrams. Even though these graphs involve only one independent variable and two countries, the insights they provide nevertheless hold for cases involving larger numbers of countries and independent variables.

Considering education as the only relevant factor in the determination of the types of services performed (the job content) within a particular occupation, how could intercountry or interindustry wage differentials be ascertained? Given that the wage differential could respond as much to educational as to country or industry variation, the objective would be to measure the latter differential in net terms. In other words, it is necessary to account for the effects of education on wage variation before determining the wage differences between countries or industries.

We can start by establishing the manner in which the level of education affects wages. In figure 2-1, the upward sloping lines suggest that higher levels of education (E representing years of education) are associated with higher pay (W equivalent to wages). Suppose that these are independent regression equations estimating the impact of education on wages for each country. Then, in order to estimate the net intercountry or interindustry differences, the comparisons should specify equal educational levels in both countries or industries, say point E_o. The wages corresponding to this level of education in figure 2-1 are W_a and W_b. Thus, the wage differential in absolute terms would be $W_a - W_b$.

In practice, it is not necessary to separate the data on wages and characteristics for each country, industry, etc., and to fit an independent equation to each set. It is possible to pool the country or industry observations. Under the assumption that the slope coefficients do not differ (figure 2-1), one basic equation is estimated from the joint data set, and a dummy variable measures the intercounty or interindustry wage differential.[11]

---

10. See Irving Kravis and Robert Lipsey, "International Price Comparisons by Regression Methods," *International Economic Review,* June 1969, pp. 234*ff.* For illustrations see Irving Kravis and Robert Lipsey, *Price Competitiveness in World Trade* (Washington, D.C.: National Bureau of Economic Research, 1971).

11. A dummy variable is used in econometrics for convenience in distinguishing among various situations. One of its initial applications, for example, was in the determination of the

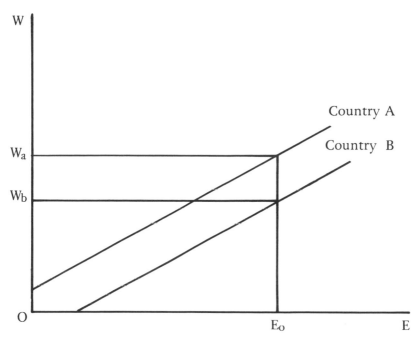

Figure 2-1. Equal wage differentials by education

By pooling, degrees of freedom are gained and greater confidence can be attached to the resulting parameters. Also the range of variation of the variables considered is amplified, which may improve both the estimation of the coefficients and the specification of the mathematical form of the relation fitted. Furthermore, pooling is simpler to handle since only one estimating equation is required rather than one separate equation for each country involved.

Figure 2-1 depicts a situation in which the absolute wage difference is the same for all possible educational levels. This implies that the slope coefficients or implicit prices of an additional year of education for the workers are the same in the two countries or industries considered. More common,

---

divergence in consumption levels before and after World War II. The variable can only take two values, usually zero or one. The former is used whenever an observation corresponding to the base case (country, industry, or whatever) is encountered, the latter whenever an observation not corresponding to the base case is considered. The number of dummy variables depends on how many cases there are to consider other than the base case. When an equation is fitted to pooled data, the coefficients of the dummy variables represent the difference between the coefficient of the particular case they represent and the base case.

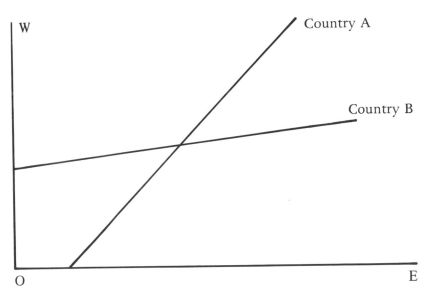

Figure 2-2. Varying wage differentials by education

however, is the situation pictured in figure 2-2, where the slopes of the equations are different in the countries in question. In this case, the wage differential varies according to the educational level. Here, the overall difference has to be determined by evaluating it at several values of E and combining these into a weighted measure.

In the situation depicted in figure 2-2, introducing a dummy variable to capture the country effect does not improve on separate country regressions because the slopes of the latter are not equal. Much better results would be obtained by fitting separate regressions in each case. However, there is an alternative procedure which retains the advantages of pooling. This method consists of fitting a single equation to pooled data, and introducing not only country dummies that measure wage differences between them in terms of intercept shifts but also dummy variables that would capture differences in the country slopes.[12] This alternative permits differences in both the intercepts and the slopes of the country or industry regression lines to be calculated from the pooled regression. Because of its convenient properties, this "flexible pooling" approach will be the principal statistical instrument utilized in the study. On occasion, however, separate equations or conventional pooling (with only intercept dummies included) will be used.

12. The first kind is called intercept dummies, and the second type, slope dummmies. For a discussion of this method see Jan Kmenta, *Elements of Econometrics* (New York: Macmillan, 1970), pp. 409–30.

Regression procedures

In order to control for heterogeneity in labor services or job content, three qualitative factors were considered: education, experience, and degree of responsibility.[13] Introducing these variables in the flexible pooling equation allows one to obtain parametric estimates of their effects on total wage variation. Once these estimates are known it is possible to obtain wage estimates for the same levels of education, experience, and responsibility across countries within given industries. Wage differentials persisting after adjusting for the qualitative variables can be considered to approximate intercountry wage differentials.

Stepwise regression was mostly used in the flexible pooling regressions. At each step an independent variable is included on a sequential basis (the selection being in order of descending contribution to the reduction of the unexplained wage variance). This procedure can be truncated when the inclusion of another independent variable (that is, a further step in the computation) does not reduce significantly the unexplained variance. As a result the effect of each independent variable, the significance of the various regression coefficients, the overall multiple coefficients of determination (R^2), and other estimates are provided at each step. Stepwise regression also facilitates study of interrelations among the independent variables.

In addition to linear equations, other forms were experimented with. In particular, double-log, semi-log, and inverse semi-log forms were also estimated to see which form fitted best. Most of these tests were of a statistical nature, while others were suggested by a priori theoretical considerations.

The basic statistical criteria used in the selection of the mathematical form of the regression equations were these: (1) the degree of explanation produced by each form, basically determined by its coefficient of determination (R^2);[14] (2) signs and significance of the coefficient in each form; (3) heteroscedasticity tests to ascertain whether and in what manner the variance of the residuals changes across the range of the independent variables.

A priori theoretical considerations suggest that forms of the equation which express wages in logarithmic terms should be preferred. Relative rather than absolute differences appear to be a more appropriate and comprehensive concept in the measurement of wage differentials. To know that

13. The operational definitions of these variables are presented in appendix 3-3.

14. The R^2, the double-log, and the inverse semi-log forms measure the ability to estimate logs of wages, while for the linear form the R^2 refers to the estimation of wages in absolute terms. To compare the values of R^2, these forms must be judged on the same grounds, either the estimation of logarithms or of absolute numbers.

Colombian wages are 20% higher than Paraguayan wages is usually more enlightening than to learn that their absolute difference is $2 an hour (a $2 difference when the base is $5 is certainly unlike a $2 difference when the base is $20). Thus, when wages are in absolute terms, the resulting differences must be related to a particular base in order to be meaningful. When the dependent variable is in logarithms the corresponding wage differences are already in relative terms.

Also, it makes more sense to minimize squares of percentage deviations about the regression function rather than squares of absolute deviations. Every deviation does not have the same importance, and the criterion for judging it should be expressed in relative rather than absolute terms. A large absolute deviation between observed and estimated values in the high-wage range should be considered less important than the same absolute deviation in the low-wage range.

Moreover, it seems possible that in many cases a constant percentage would be a good approximation of the net wage differentials among countries or industries. The same cannot be said for a fixed absolute difference. Finally, there is good reason to believe that wages, like other income variables, are lognormally distributed.[15] On this account, a logarithmic specification of wages as the dependent variable should also be superior to a linear one.

Such a priori theoretical considerations favor the double-log and inverse semi-log forms, in which the dependent variable is in logarithmic terms.[16] The statistical tests mentioned previously also indicated that the double-log and inverse semi-log forms were usually superior; thus they were the forms generally used in the regression analysis.

Statistical problems encountered in applying hedonic techniques

Several statistical problems had to be confronted in the regression experiments. One of them was the possible presence of multicollinearity or intercorrelation among the independent variables included, as a result of which coefficients tend to be distorted and have high standard errors, while the overall coefficient of determination may be inflated. In particular, a combination of high R^2 with low t statistics may signal significant intercorrelation.

Generally this was not encountered in this regression work. In general, it

15. J. Aitchison and J. A. C. Brown, *The Lognormal Distribution* (Cambridge: Cambridge University Press, 1969), pp. 101–2 and 119–20; and Martin Bronfenbrenner, *Income Distribution Theory* (New York: Aldine-Atherton, 1971), chap. 3.

16. In chapter 3 of John Johnson, *Econometric Methods* (New York: McGraw-Hill, 1972), these forms are reviewed.

was found that the simple coefficients of determination among the independent variables were rarely above 0.30. If a coefficient was above 0.50, one of the variables involved was dropped from the model.

The multicollinearity problem sometimes exists for a set of independent variables in combination, though it is not apparent when the variables are considered in pairs. It was felt, however, that the small additional precision to be gained in testing further for this problem (apart from the indications provided by the R^2 and the t ratios) was not worth the effort.[17]

One consideration was that unless the degree of variation in the sample for both the dependent and independent variables is sizable, the overall correlation between them is not likely to be large. Because dummies are abundantly used in this study, and many of the other independent variables are expressed in categorical form (that is, in terms of levels), the statistical results obtained may be affected by their lack of variation.[18]

As will be seen later, most of the regression equations do not seem affected by this problem, which is demonstrated by the generally high explanatory levels attained. On the other hand, this factor may cause the low significance and wrong signs of some of the regression coefficients estimated.[19]

A more important cause of wrong signs and low significance of the regression coefficients may be that, as a result of the size and characteristics of the sample (discussed later in this chapter), few degrees of freedom remain. Also, intercorrelation among the independent variables may give rise to some of the unexpected signs.[20]

Tests were performed to evaluate the importance of incorrect signs, generally finding that the error was not a serious one. Furthermore, when there are complex relations among the independent variables, it may be theoretically and empirically justified to leave the wrong coefficients in as a more precise representation of reality.[21] Therefore, instead of eliminating the variable in question, it was left in the estimating equations.

17. See the explanation of Bartlett's test in D. E. Farrod and R. R. Glober, "Multicollinearity in Regression Analysis: The Problem Revisited," *Review of Economics and Statistics,* February 1967, pp. 102, 107.

18. On these points see Mordecai Ezekiel and Karl Fox, *Methods of Correlation and Regression Analysis* (New York: John Wiley, 1959), chap. 17, pp. 129–30 and 197–98.

19. Daniel Suits, *Statistics* (Chicago: Rand McNally, 1963), pp. 116–17 and 119–20.

20. In general, variables with incorrect signs in the estimated equations were found to have the expected signs in their coefficients of simple correlation with the dependent variable (wages).

21. See Zvi Griliches, "Hedonic Price Indexes for Automobiles: An Econometric Analysis of Quality Change," in *Price Indexes and Quality Change,* ed. Zvi Griliches (Cambridge, Mass.: Harvard University Press, 1971).

Unfortunately, not all the variables important in the explanation of wage differentials could be included in this study. This raises the possibility that some of the variables selected may be acting as proxies for the excluded ones, in ways which will be difficult to discover. The regression coefficients would then be affected, making it difficult to discern the effects of the independent variables included. Not much could be done about this problem, this being one of the limitations of the study. However, the most important determinants of wage differentials in Latin America are believed to have been covered.

Another important problem in the context of hedonic regression analysis is the apportionment of the total wage variation among the factors included; basically the qualitative characteristics determining labor skills or job content and the country, industry, or firm variables. It should be clear that such apportionment might have to be somewhat arbitrary. The significance of some of the coefficients involved may be in doubt, and, given that only significant coefficients should be retained in the regression equation, a decision rule concerning significance seems to be needed. This was defined in the comparative chapters of the study to be the 10% level of significance. The consequences of this rule are especially important in the case of the slope and intercept dummies, which are the variables ultimately determining the effects of country, industry, and similar variables.

Two situations have to be distinguished here. One of them would involve only intercept dummies (as in figure 2-1), with wage differentials being uniform throughout the range of variation of the independent variables. The other is characterized by the presence of intercept and slope dummies, with the wage differences varying at different values of the independent variables. The latter would hold when flexible pooling techniques are being used, as is most common in this study.

In the first case the determination of the particular net wage differential is quite simple: the intercept dummies measure it directly. When the qualitative variables related to labor skills or job content are normalized across countries or industries, the only differences among them are given by the significant intercept dummy coefficients. In the double-log and inverse semi-log forms the dependent variable is in logarithms, so the intercept dummy would represent a uniform percentage difference in wages. In the case of the semi-log or the arithmetic formula the intercept dummy would express a constant absolute differential, given that the dependent variable is in absolute terms.

On the other hand, whenever slope dummies appear in combination with intercept dummies (see figure 2-2), it is necessary to establish a basis for comparison. This is because in this situation the differential would vary within the range of the independent variables. In this case various sets of normalized values of the qualitative variables should be used. Because there are indications that wages are lognormally distributed, quartile values of the qualitative variables were used in this study to measure wage differences.[22] Such wage differences were weighted and averaged later in order to express the results unambiguously in terms of a single scale. Sample observations were used in estimating the quartile values.

When using intercept and slope dummies for each set of normalized values, the wage differences among the cases (countries, industries, and so on) will be dictated by the significant intercept and slope dummy coefficients. Thus the decision about the significance of these coefficients has an important effect upon the wage differentials. As in the first situation, depending on the specification of the dependent variable, the differences will be in relative or absolute terms at each set of normalized values of the independent variables. However, these wage differentials would have to be weighted and averaged in order to determine the overall intercountry or interindustry wage differential.

22. See Aitchison and Brown, *The Lognormal Distribution*, chapter 2; and Bronfenbrenner, *Income Distribution Theory*, chapter 3.

Chapter 3. Characteristics and scope
of the wage survey

Statistics in the LAFTA countries are generally in a state of underdevelopment. This is particularly true of labor statistics. The data necessary for the measurement of interindustry, interfirm, and other wage differentials, even in gross terms, are scarce. For intercountry comparisons the problem is more serious because the available data are more heterogeneous.[1] Thus, it was essential to conduct a special survey to obtain appropriate data for this study.

The data collection effort was carefully planned. Based on previous experience with similar surveys, the Instituto de Pesquisas Econômicas of the Universidade de São Paulo prepared and tested a preliminary set of procedures for the wage survey. All the ECIEL institutes collaborating on the project attended a workshop to review this proposal. A revised set of survey procedures was adopted at this workshop, which the institutes tested in their respective countries. The participants met again in another workshop, from which a final set of procedures emerged. Most of the surveys were undertaken in 1967, with the questionnaires and manuals used following the basic design approved by the institutes.

The survey work in the field was afflicted by problems in virtually all countries. In some cases, the first attempt was a partial or total loss, because the desired information was either missing or unreliable, and a new or follow-up survey had to be implemented. Long delays resulted from the lackluster collaboration of many firms. All the data refer to the same date (November 1966), irrespective of the moment at which each survey was undertaken. The period of reference chosen was considered to be as normal as could be expected in a study involving several industries and countries. It should be borne in mind that Latin American manufacturing, and especially its modern sector, has been less affected by cyclical fluctuations than the rest of the economy. In terms of the overall performance of the national

1. For a picture of the difficulties faced, see John R. Eriksson, "Wage Structures and Economic Development in Selected Latin American Countries, A Comparative Analysis" (Ph.D. diss., University of California, Berkeley, 1966).

economies, the most salient points were the fact that 1966 was a year of zero or negative growth for Argentina, slack growth for Brazil (manufacturing grew steadily during the first half of the year, tapered off during the third quarter, and leveled off entirely in the last quarter), and relatively strong growth in Bolivia, Mexico, and Peru.[2]

Selection of industries

As stated previously, the study was limited to a few manufacturing industries.

Several criteria were used in selecting these industries:

1. As far as possible, they were to be representative of the manufacturing sector as a whole, especially with respect to wages, occupations, and the rest of the data collected in the survey.

2. Together, the industries selected had to account for a significant portion of the employment contributed and value added by the manufacturing sector.

3. The industries on which the intercountry comparisons were principally based had to be present in every LAFTA country.

4. The industries had to be large enough to comply with the requirements of the survey on number of firms covered.

Nine industries were selected by these criteria: textiles, pharmaceuticals, metallurgy, lumber, heavy household appliances, tires, automobile assembly, paper products, and vegetable oils. The international comparisons mainly involved the first three industries, and these were covered in every country. Recognizing the inappropriateness of surveying some of the other industries mentioned in each country, substitutions and omissions were permitted in this group.[3] Table 3-1 presents a list of the industries covered in each country.

The importance of the industries selected in terms of value added and employment should be noted. In a static sense, the relative significance of these industries can be measured in terms of the ratios O_j/O_i and N_j/N_i, where O stands for value added, N for employment, j for sampled industries, and i for all industries. Tables 3-2 and 3-3 present these ratios for the different LAFTA nations in selected years, including the year of the survey.

The three main industries (textiles, metallurgy, and pharmaceuticals), accounted for about 25% of manufacturing value added in 1966 in most countries (table 3-2), and their share has been generally increasing. The

2. U.N. Economic Commission for Latin America, *Economic Survey of Latin America, 1966* (New York: United Nations, 1968).

3. In certain countries some of these industries were not representative or sufficiently important, and they were replaced by other industries.

Table 3-1. Industries covered in the wage studies

Industries	Argentina	Bolivia[a]	Brazil	Chile	Colombia	Ecuador	Mexico	Paraguay	Peru	Uruguay	Venezuela
Textiles	X	X	X	X	X	X	X	X	X	X	X
Pharmaceuticals	X	X	X	X	X	X	X	X	X	X	X
Metallurgy	X		X	X	X	X	X	X	X	X	X
Vegetable oils	X		X			X	X	X	X	X	X
Lumber	X		X	X	X	X	X	X	X	X	
Automobile assembly	X		X	X	X	X	X	X	X		X
Heavy household appliances	X		X	X			X		X	X	X
Tires	X				X		X		X	X	X
Paper products	X		X				X		X	X	X
Meat packing								X			
Sugar								X			
Citrus fruit								X			
Glassware				X	X						
Beer					X				X		
Cement					X						X
Petroleum derivatives					X						

[a] Bolivia joined the project at a late date, which partly explains why so few industries were surveyed in that country. Another factor was the rudimentary nature of its manufacturing sector.

Table 3-2. Ratio of value added in sample industries over value added in manufacturing (percentages)[a]

Country	Three main industries[b]	Sample industries	Country	Three main industries[b]	Sample industries
Argentina			Mexico		
1960	49.36	72.71	1960	31.48	55.38
1966	50.40	72.80	1966	32.46	63.46
Bolivia			Paraguay		
	n.a.	n.a.	1960	n.a.	n.a.
Brazil			1966	24.99[f]	66.06[f]
1960	37.30[c]	55.20[c]	Peru		
1966	42.03[d]	60.07[d]	1960	21.29[f]	60.47[f]
Chile			1966	24.65[d]	57.09[d]
1960	27.49[e]	37.21[e]	Uruguay		
1966	28.94	39.10	1960	22.16	35.35
Colombia			1966	24.24	34.01
1960	29.41	57.06	Venezuela		
1966	29.95	56.01	1960	15.14	25.60
Ecuador			1966	16.68	30.85
1960	22.21[e]	24.01[e]			
1966	21.77	24.22			

SOURCES: Banco Central de la República Argentina, *Suplemento del Boletín Estadístico*, 1 (Jan. 1971); OAS: Instituto Interamericano de Estadística, *America en Cifras: 1967 y 1970; Situación Económica: 2 Industrias* (for Bolivia, Chile, Ecuador, Paraguay, and Peru); Instituto Brasilerino de Geografía e Estatística, *Anuario Estatística do Brasil: 1969*; Banco Central del Uruguay, *Producto e Ingreso Nacional* (1971); United Nations, *The Growth of World Industry*: Vol. I. *General Industrial Statistics 1960–1968* (1967, 1969 editions), for Colombia; Banco Central de Venezuel, *Informe Económico: 1969*; Banco de México S.A., *Cuentas Nacionales y Acervos de Capital Consolidados y por Tipo de Actividad Económica 1950–1967* (1971); OAS: Instituto Interamericano de Estadística, *El Esfuerzo Interno y las Necesidades de Financiamiento Externo para el Desarrollo de Venezuela* (1971).

n.a. = Data not available.

[a] Because of the unavailability of sufficiently disarregated data there is a general upward bias in our ratios, which results from attributing to the industries selected the figures corresponding to broader industrial classifications. This is especially marked in the case of the pharmaceutical industry and for Argentina and Brazil.

[b] Textiles, pharmaceuticals, and metallurgy.

[c] Data for 1959.

[d] Data for 1965.

[e] Data for 1964.

[f] Data for 1963.

Table 3-3. Ratio of employment in sample industries over employment in manufacturing[a]

Country	Three main industries[b]	Sample industries	Country	Three main industries[b]	Sample industries
Argentina			Mexico		
1960	25.45	52.16	1960	n.a.	n.a.
1966	26.52	53.01	1966	28.24[e]	46.95[e]
Bolivia			Paraguay		
1960	n.a.	n.a.	1960	n.a.	n.a.
1966	19.42	19.42	1966	19.23[f]	58.11[f]
Brazil			Peru		
1960	31.91[c]	46.79[c]	1960	25.90[f]	41.90[f]
1966	29.07	45.75	1966	28.65[e]	44.17[e]
Chile			Uruguay		
1960	31.92[d]	44.18[d]	1960	n.a.	n.a.
1966	31.21	43.68	1966	25.51[f]	35.85[f]
Colombia			Venezuela		
1960	29.98	50.33	1960	6.35	17.63
1966	29.69	49.18	1966	9.67	24.40
Ecuador					
1960	34.52[d]	38.90[d]			
1966	32.98	37.22			

SOURCES: Same as for table 3-2, except for Mexico and Uruguay, where data was obtained from OAS, *América en Cifras*, 1967 and 1970.

n.a. = Data not available.

[a] Because of the unavailability of sufficiently disaggregated data, there is a general upward bias in these ratios. See previous table for further details.

[b] Textiles, pharmaceuticals, and metallurgy.

[c] Data for 1959.

[d] Data for 1964.

[e] Data for 1965.

[f] Data for 1963.

share of manufacturing value added for all the industries in the survey varied more widely, because the coverage was somewhat dissimilar. The average was around 30% with the trend increasing more sharply.

Most of the industry statistics were taken from the OAS publication, *America en Cifras,* and thus the definition of each industry across countries is generally comparable. However, for a few countries (Argentina, Brazil, Colombia, Mexico, and Uruguay), other sources had to be used, and there is no assurance that the definitions in the latter coincide among each other or with the OAS publication. Data on value added for the specific industries surveyed were unavailable. As an alternative, figures referring to generally broader industrial classifications are presented.[4] Although this entailed overestimating the industries' importance, the figures were deemed acceptable as approximations.

The measure of importance of the industries covered is usually higher in terms of employment (see table 3-3), being close to 30% for the three main industries and over 40% for all the industries covered in the survey. This ratio, however, has been decreasing over time.[5] As with value added, these statistics are to a certain extent noncomparable and overestimate the importance of the sampled industries.

It is also important to be aware of the growth record of the industries sampled relative to that of the overall manufacturing sector. Tables 3-4 and 3-5 summarize this record for recent years with respect to value added and employment, respectively. As can be seen, value added in the sampled industries has grown as fast as all the others sampled in terms of value added but less in terms of employment.

Selection of firms

Given the imperfect conditions prevailing in the labor market of LAFTA countries, differences in labor productivity among firms can be expected to contribute largely to wage differentials. These labor productivity differences are caused by several factors, such as varying capital-labor ratios and levels of technology. Although the latter variables were not probed, their influence was isolated through appropriate selection of the firms interviewed.[6] In order to minimize labor productivity differences among them,

4. This problem mostly affected the figures for Argentina and Brazil, but also in some measure all other countries with the possible exception of Venezuela.

5. As just noted, in terms of value added the opposite holds. This suggests that the rate of increase in labor productivity in the industries studied has been higher than in manufacturing as a whole.

6. This expectation was afterwards proven right in another ECIEL project specifically designed for comparisons of technological efficiency and productivity. This research effort was

Table 3-4. Annual percentage rate of growth in value added for sample industries and for total manufacturing, 1960-66

Country	Three main industries	All industries sampled	Total manufacturing
Argentina	5.3	5.0	5.0
Bolivia	n.a.	n.a.	n.a.
Brazil	15.1	16.3	15.0
Chile	19.5	19.1	16.4
Colombia	20.0	n.a.	14.8
Ecuador	13.6	16.9	14.8
Mexico	8.3	10.2	7.7
Paraguay	n.a.	n.a.	n.a.
Peru	21.0	21.0	12.8
Uruguay	2.3	0.2	0.9
Venezuela	9.1	10.7	7.4

SOURCES: See table 3-2.

Table 3-5. Annual percentage rate of growth in employment for sampled industries and for total manufacturing, 1960–66

Country	Three main industries	All industries sampled	Total manufacturing
Argentina	1.2	0.7	0.5
Bolivia	n.a.	n.a.	n.a.
Brazil	0.5	3.0	4.3
Chile	2.5	3.5	3.6
Colombia	3.3	3.1	3.5
Ecuador	3.6	3.7	6.0
Mexico	n.a.	n.a.	n.a.
Paraguay	n.a.	n.a.	n.a.
Peru	5.7	0.2	2.5
Uruguay	n.a.	n.a.	n.a.
Venezuela	11.4	9.7	3.9

SOURCES: See table 3-3.

only the most efficient and largest firms in each industry and country were to be selected.[7]

Moreover, since the study focused on integration, an effort was made to include in the survey firms that are already exporting or with export capabilities. However, a requirement common to both cases would appear to be that the firms market their products nationwide within their respective countries. These firms would usually be located in or near the industrial centers of the various countries, with the exception of those belonging to industries whose location patterns are determined by proximity to the source of raw materials. For this reason, the surveys were concentrated on the principal industrial centers in each country, usually the capital cities and sometimes one or two other relatively large cities.

Every institute was to survey at least nine firms with the characteristics just outlined in each of the three industries used for international comparisons (textiles, metallurgy, and pharmaceuticals). If less than nine firms met these requirements, all of them were to be surveyed. The same procedures were followed in the other six industries, except that the number of firms required in each was only five.

Unfortunately these goals could not be attained due to collection difficulties. Hence, the number of firms covered in the various countries generally fell short of the target, as is shown in table 3-6. However, since the markets of LAFTA countries are quite small, being usually dominated by a few modern firms,[8] the firms surveyed are felt to represent an important part of employment in the industries considered. Although it was impossible to obtain value-added data, most of these firms were the most modern and efficient in the industry, and their labor productivities would be expected to exceed respective industry averages.

Table 3-7 presents the percentages of total employment in each industry accounted for by the respondent firms. Because employment in each industry is overestimated, as explained before, the percentages underestimate

---

discontinued because of lack of cooperation by the firms. See Peter Knight, "Problemas de la Comparación Internacional de la Eficiencia Económica . . . La Experiencia de ECIEL," *Ensayos ECIEL 1,* (1975).

7. The prevailing opinion is that the largest plants also have higher capital-labor ratios and more up-to-date technology and innovative management, thus making them more modern. Hence, size, efficiency, labor productivity, and modernity are usually related. See Suzanne Paine, "Wage Differentials in the Japanese Manufacturing Sector," *Oxford Economic Papers* (July 1971).

8. On these points see Joseph Grunwald, Miguel Wionczek, and Martin Carnoy, *Latin American Economic Integration and United States Policy* (Washington, D.C.: Brookings Institution, 1972).

Table 3-6. Number of firms in the wage survey by industry and country

Industry	Country											
	Arg	Bol	Bra	Chi	Col	Ecu	Mex	Par	Per	Uru	Ven	Total
Textiles	10	7	6	9	12	10	4	4	9	6	2	79
Pharmaceuticals	10	4	6	9	8	4	n.a.	2	9	8	9	77
Metallurgy	9	–	8	9	10	5	8	1	9	7	6	64
Vegetable oils	6	–	1	–	–	6	n.a.	3	1	1	3	21
Lumber	5	–	2	6	1	4	n.a.	2	5	1	–	26
Automobile assembly	5	–	5	–	–	–	n.a.	1	4	–	3	18
Heavy household appliances	4	–	5	9	–	–	n.a.	–	3	4	4	29
Tires	5	–	–	–	1	–	n.a.	–	1	1	3	11
Paper products	4	–	3	–	–	–	n.a.	–	4	1	3	15
Meat packing	–	–	–	–	–	–	–	3	–	–	–	3
Sugar	–	–	–	–	–	–	–	3	–	–	–	3
Citrus fruit	–	–	–	–	–	–	–	1	–	–	–	1
Glassware	–	–	–	5	3	–	–	–	–	–	–	8
Beer	–	–	–	–	1	–	–	–	1	–	–	2
Cement	–	–	–	–	1	–	–	–	–	–	2	3
Petroleum derivatives	–	–	–	–	1	–	–	–	–	–	–	1
Total	58	11	36	47	38	29	12	20	46	29	35	361

n.a. = Data not available.

Table 3-7. Percentage of total industry employment in firms surveyed, by country, 1966[a]

Industry	Country									
	Arg	Bol	Bra	Chi	Col	Ecu	Par	Per	Uru	Ven
Textiles	20.7	46.2	4.4	22.6	30.0	57.7	96.6	20.5	10.7	11.3
Pharmaceuticals	8.5	41.9	28.3	2.0	7.7	42.0	6.3	19.8	12.5	17.7
Metallurgy	16.2	–	7.2	16.6	56.7	46.4	20.1	45.8	27.6	12.5
Vegetable oils	1.3	–	1.1	–	–	32.4	17.7	5.3	2.4	10.6
Lumber	1.1	–	1.9	3.1	7.2	56.3	18.1	21.5	6.1	–
Automobile assembly	7.4	–	73.8	–	–	–	5.1	28.6	–	12.8
Heavy household appliances	12.1	–	6.0	84.5	–	–	–	30.3	10.3	16.9
Tires	62.5	–	–	–	15.9	–	–	35.9	98.8	46.3
Paper products	8.5	–	2.5	–	–	–	–	15.6	–	14.6
Meat packing	–	–	–	–	–	–	56.8	–	–	–
Sugar	–	–	–	–	–	–	9.3	–	–	–
Citrus fruit	–	–	–	–	–	–	2.6	–	–	–
Glassware	–	–	–	9.4	10.6	–	–	–	–	–
Beer	–	–	–	–	7.4	–	–	16.3	–	–
Cement	–	–	–	–	1.6	–	–	–	–	12.4
Petroleum derivatives	–	–	–	–	17.1	–	–	–	–	–

SOURCES: See table 3-3.

[a] For the same reason that the ratios were biased upward in tables 3-2 and 3-3, the results here reflect a downward bias, because the total employment figures in each industry are inflated.

sample representation in each industry. On the average, the three main industries covered 27% of total employment, while for all the industries sampled the ratio was 25%.

Occupations covered and wage data obtained

In manufacturing, imperfect competition generally rules in the labor and products markets in Latin America. The price for labor in the same occupation and with equivalent skills or job content differs among firms within a particular industry. Thus, since each firm often has a different input price for the same labor factor, it was deemed necessary to gather information at the firm level rather than for each industry as a whole.

It was believed that wage information could be more easily and accurately obtained from firm records than from employee interviews. While it is not clear that the data on occupation and job content should be gathered from the employer instead of the employee, seeking the necessary information from employees would have required increasing the required number of interviews and including a larger number of qualitative variables in the determination of labor skills or job content, which would have been much more expensive. Also, with employer data it is possible to concentrate on the most important factors without distoring the effect of other variables on labor skills or job content.[9]

In each firm, minimum, average, and maximum wages were requested for every position. (The questionnaire is shown in appendix 3-1.) This information was obtained from the personnel manager (or an executive with similar responsibilities) in each of the firms.

The minimum salaries obtained correspond to the starting salaries of workers who could adequately perform the tasks required by the particular position; thus apprentices and trainees were excluded. These generally were the salaries of the lowest paid workers in those positions. Average wages constituted estimates of mean pay for each position. Maximum salaries referred to the highest grade in the pay scale of a particular position; these usually corresponded to the salaries received by the highest paid workers in the position.

9. There are other reasons for preferring employers as sources. One of them is that they usually have a more adequate knowledge of the levels of the qualitiative variables than are required to properly fill a particular position. An employee might not even be aware of the degree of responsibility necessary and might not even be able to judge his own. In addition, the characteristics of a certain employee may only assure him of a transitory stay in the position in question, and should not be taken as an indication of its job content. Finally, the employee may have strong reasons to conceal his true levels of qualitative variables in question.

Two different wage concepts are used in this study: labor cost and net salary or take-home pay. The latter was defined as straight wages (excluding overtime and shift premiums) plus fringe benefits received periodically by the employee minus social security deductions. Examples of fringe benefits are end-of-year bonuses, family allowances, and incentive premiums. Labor cost is defined as straight wages plus all kinds of fringe benefits, whether paid out regularly to the employees or not, i.e., employer contributions to the pension plan, unemployment compensation, accident and disability insurance.

It would be useful to find out if wage differentials measured in terms of labor costs differ significantly from those calculated on the basis of take-home pay. If not, the collection of data for the analysis of wage structure could be greatly simplified. Of course, each has its own special relevance. While labor cost is more useful in the study of production efficiency and trade, take-home pay is more related to the study of labor migration, while also providing valuable information about labor incomes, their distribution, and the potential demand they generate.

As stated previously, a problem affecting previous wage structure studies, especially those attempting intercountry comparisons, has been the heterogeneity of the labor services compared. For this reason, this study goes beneath occupations and uses the concept of positions instead. Occupation and position are not the same thing. There usually are several positions within an occupation; for example, there are different kinds and grades of lathe operators, typists, bookkeepers, etc.[10]

The characteristics and responsibilities of some of these positions were carefully defined to ensure even greater comparability, namely, those positions expected to be found in every firm, industry, and country. These could very well be called key positions due to their commonness, and because they appear to be good indicators of the wage characteristics of a large number of other positions.

The key positions were selected to cover a fair variety of job content, from those requiring little education and experience to those requiring substantial amounts. Obviously, another requirement for a position to be included in the survey was the ease with which it could be specified. The key positions selected and their descriptions are presented in appendix 3-2.

In order to make the surveys representative and broad ranging, other positions were also included, which were not predetermined or described in the questionnaire. It was agreed that the institutes would select positions

10. On this point see Eriksson, "Wage Structures and Economic Development," pp. 134–45.

to make the sample representative at the firm and industry levels in their respective countries. For this second class of positions, a job description was requested from the employers in the questionnaire (appendix 3-1, part II).

All positions covered by the survey were classified into two categories: clerical and production jobs. The pay differentials between these two kinds of personnel approximate those between white-collar and blue-collar workers. The importance of this differential for developing countries has been amply documented, and it is hoped that future research on this topic could be based on data generated in these wage surveys.[11] The same holds true of skill differentials, given the various skill levels represented in the sample.

Job content expressed in terms of qualitative variables

In this study, labor skill or job content is kept unchanged across industries, countries, and the like. That is, wages are normalized or standardized to correspond to uniform job content in terms of education, experience, and degree of responsibility. The differentials among countries, industries, and so forth obtained in this fashion are compared with those taken from traditionally oriented wage comparisons (in which wages are averaged by industry and position) in order to ascertain the extent to which the results of the alternative procedures differ.

Education, experience, and degree of responsibility were used to standardize job content because they were closely related to job content and were relatively easy to qualify. Also, firms use these variables in evaluating the qualitative requirements of their positions, and for a finer discrimination of job content within them.

This entails the definition of these variables in categorical form, with each level representing a different degree of achievement.[12] These levels are related to the minimal requirements that an individual would have to satisfy in order to perform adequately the tasks required in his job.

Although there might be discrepancies between the required levels and the actual characteristics of the employees, it is to be expected that the evaluation of requirements by the personnel manager would closely reflect the quality of personnel employed in the various positions. Lags may ap-

11. See Koji Taira, "Wage Differentials in Developing Countries: A Survey of Findings," *International Labor Review,* March–June 1966; Lloyd G. Reynolds, *Relative Earnings and Manpower Allocation in Developing Economies,* Yale University Economic Growth Center Paper 134 (New Haven, Conn: 1969); and Melvin W. Reder, *Labor in a Growing Economy* (New York: Wiley, 1958).

12. Ruy Leme, *Administração Salarial,* mimeographed (São Paulo: Universidade de São Paulo, 1970), chap. 3. This method of job evaluation is known as the points system.

pear, but they are probably corrected from time to time by adjusting either the salaries or the employer's requirements.[13]

Employers can be expected to hire only those workers that meet or exceed their requirements (in terms of education, experience, etc.) for particular positions and jobs, and the remuneration paid is tied to these requirements. If the particular characteristics of an employee exceed these requirements, he does not get a higher salary, unless the job content is changed to fit his characteristics.

In many cases, the qualitative levels measured in the survey cover several values of the factors in question. A particular educational level, for example, will comprise more than one value in terms of years of formal education; for instance, level 5 is defined to mean 7 to 8 years of formal education. This reflects the fact that for certain qualitative factors, each position and job in a firm is generally related to a range of qualitative values rather than to a specific one. In evaluating the requirements of a particular set of tasks, firms usually define ranges of acceptable values for these factors.[14] This results from the fact that a particular set of tasks usually allows for some flexibility in requirements. Also, since the combinations of these main qualitative factors probably differ among job applicants, it is convenient for personnel policies to be elastic in the definition of levels.

A manual, as well as a set of questionnaires and instructions, was distributed to the institutes well in advance of the surveys. Based on this common core, each institute decided whether and in what ways it would supplement the questionnaire. Then training sessions were conducted in each country for the staff participating in the wage surveys.

After the firms had been chosen, contacts were made with their personnel managers or executives performing similar duties, and interviews arranged. The interviewer's main objective was to select, with the personnel manager, the positions and jobs for which data would be requested. The firm's requirements for each position and job, in terms of the qualitative variables included in the surveys, were obtained afterwards. The interviewer would then attempt to express that information according to the

13. An evaluation manual for each of these variables, together with a set of basic instructions for the survey, is in appendix 3-3. The same manual and instructions were used in every country.

14. For references on these and previous points, see Eriksson, "Wage Structures and Economic Development," pp. 136–46; Walter Fogel, "Job Rate Changes: A Theoretical and Empirical Analysis," *Industrial and Labor Relations Review,* July 1964; J. Mey, "Wage Structure and Organization Structure," E. Kosiol, "Theory of Wage Forms," and G. Hildebrand, "External Influences and the Determination of the Internal Wage Structure," in *Internal Wage Structure,* comp. J. Mey (Amsterdam: North-Holland, 1963).

Table 3-8. Levels of educational requirements for a particular industry in a specific country by position and firm

Position	Firm		
	E_1	Average	Range
1			
2			
3			
4			
.			
.			
.			
.			
M			

levels of the qualitative factors defined in appendix 3-3, if possible with the personnel manager. Finally, the corresponding wage data were obtained directly from the personnel manager, and questionnaires were left so that the rest of the information would be filled in. In many cases a second interview, and at times a third, proved necessary to obtain additional data and to check what had already been supplied.

After they were collected, some consistency checks were performed on the data. Special care was taken in checking the evaluation of the positions in terms of their qualitative requirements. The levels of the various positions were compared to ensure that the evaluations done separately were compatible with each other. The collaboration of the personnel managers was also requested at this stage. The main purpose of such checks was to ensure a successful blending of the job evaluation systems of the various firms with the uniform manual used in the project.

As a final consistency check, bivariate tables were constructed in which the rankings of the qualitative variables were classified by position and firm within each industry. Table 3-8 illustrates the format of these tables. In general, no problems were found at this stage, so that no further information or clarification had to be requested from the firms.

Appendix 3-1. Latin American
wage survey questionnaire

I. Job evaluation form

Latin-American Wage Survey Country _____ Date _____ Industrial Sector _____

Information about the firm Firm _____ Main products _____ Number of employees in the firm _____

Address _____

City _____ State or province _____

Type of position	Code	Position	Factor levels			Number of employees in position	Wage		
			Education	Experience	Initiative		Minimum	Mean	Maximum
Administrative	A-1	File clerk							
	A-2	Typist							
	A-3	Invoice clerk							
	A-4	Accounting clerk							
	A-5	Cashier							
	A-6								
	A-7								
	A-8								
	A-9								
	A-10								
	A-11								
Production	P-1	Janitor							
	P-2	Machinist							
	P-3	Lathe operator							
	P-4	Maintenance electrician							
	P-5	Inexperienced engineer							
	P-6	Truck driver							
	P-7	Foreman							
	P-8								
	P-9								
	P-10								
	P-11								
	P-12								

II. Description of non-key positions

Administrative

Code A-6   Position:
Description:

Code A-7   Position:
Description:

Code A-8   Position:
Description:

Code A-9   Position:
Description:

Code A-10   Position:
Description:

Code A-11   Position:
Description:

Production

Code P-8   Position:
Description:

Code P-9   Position:
Description:

Code P-10   Position:
Description:

Code P-11   Position:
Description:

Code P-12   Position:
Description:

III. Other Relevant Firm Information

1. Characteristics of the firm

Firm _____ Industrial sector _____

Address _____ City _____

State or Prov. _____ Country _____

Location: Urban ☐   Rural ☐

Nature of the firm's equity: Private ☐   Public ☐   Mixed ☐

Origin of the Firm's Equity: Exclusively ☐   Predominiantly ☐
                               National   National

                               Exclusively ☐   Predominantly ☐
                               Foreign   Foreign

Date at which the firm was established at the above location _____

Distribution of employees by type: Administrative _____

                                     Production _____

                                     Total _____

Main products _____

2. Economic aspects of the firm

Sales in 1966 _____

Book value (equity + reserves + undistributed profits)_____

3. Social security contributions and other fringe benefits paid by the firm in 1966

Type	Firm disbursements	Percentage of total disbursement
Required by law	____	____
Not required by law	____	____
Total	____	100%

4. Distribution of various wages components in 1966

Straight wages   _____

Bonuses and other incentive payments   _____

Family Allowances   _____

Total A _____

Social security contributions of the firm B _____

Social security contributions of the employee C _____

Labor cost $(A + B)$ _____

Net wages $(A - C)$ _____

5. How many unions are accredited with the firm? Which are the respective employee categories covered?

Union	Employee category	No. of employees
_____	_____	_____
_____	_____	_____
_____	_____	_____

How long will the contracts which have determined the firm's present wage structure be effective? _____

Appendix 3-2. Description of key positions

Administrative (A)

A-1. *Filing clerk*. Under immediate supervision, the file clerk is responsible for coding simple administrative documents, such as mail, reports, etc. These documents are then to be filed in ad hoc portfolios or compartments.

A-2. *Typist*. Under indirect supervision, the typist is responsible for transcribing drafts, memoranda, and other documents. He or she also writes and types standard documents such as file cards, requisitions, etc.

A-3. *Invoice clerk*. Under indirect supervision, the invoice clerk is responsible for carrying out the computations relevant for the invoices or products sold. In this he or she must follow price catalogues and estimate the taxes on products sold according to tax rate abstracts. Finally, he or she must check and sometimes type the invoices.

A-4. *Accounting clerk*. Following the accounting system of the firm, the accounting clerk is responsible for classifying all documents to be entered in the accounting records. He or she is to make the entries of the documents to be coded in the accounting files. Periodically, he or she is to aid in reconciling the firm's accounts and, when necessary, make relatively simple reports on the movements in special accounts.

A-5. *Cashier*. Following rules predetermined by the firm, the cashier is responsible for checking the cash balance books, verifying the movements registered in them. He or she is supposed to keep track of the movements in the cash accounts, checking deposits and withdrawals. He or she is to control the amount of cash on hand and in banks, issuing a daily statement about this matter for the superiors' information.

Production (P)

P-1. *Janitor*. Under immediate supervision, the janitor is to carry out simple jobs and clean offices. He or she is to wipe dust from office desks and furniture; to sweep, polish, and clean floors; to clean bathrooms, washstands, windows, etc. He or she is to empty ashtrays and wastepaper baskets. He or she performs no work out of the office, nor engages in any heavy work.

P-2. *Machinist.* Under immediate supervision, the machinist is responsible for operating industrial machines while they are working. However, the machinist is not responsible for maintaining, preparing, or adjusting the machine. When work is interrupted, the machinist is to seek guidance from the supervisor.

P-3. *Lathe operator.* This employee is responsible for preparing and adjusting the lathe for specific operations. The lathe operator consults designs and other technical specifications related to the operations performed. He or she verifies the dimensions of the part being made by means of precision instruments. Also, he or she is to solve small problems related to the functioning of the machine.

P-4. *Maintenance electrician.* Under indirect supervision, the maintenance electrician is to provide repair and maintenance services related to the use of electric energy throughout the factory. This is accomplished by following general instructions from a superior and by consulting factory design installations. This employee is responsible for providing repair and maintenance service for motors and other electric equipment, such as switches, circuit breakers, transformers, relays, etc. When necessary, following instructions or technical designs, he is to carry out and guide the electrical work required in the installations of new industrial equipment.

P-5. *Engineer (trainee).* Under the supervision and guidance of an experienced engineer, this employee must carry out the technical duties inherent to this professional specialization. These activities are to serve a training purpose.

P-6. *Truck driver.* Under general supervision, the truck driver is to perform routine jobs, driving light-powered vehicles having a capacity of up to three tons. Duties would include the following:

1. Transportation of equipment, material, supplies, or persons.
2. Assistance in the loading and unloading of the vehicle.
3. Routine jobs operating elevator hoists, light rollers, or agricultural tractors.
4. Other jobs of a similar nature.

P-7. *Foreman.* Under general supervision, the foreman is to distribute and control the work of a small group of sub-foremen, who in turn supervise a large number of semiskilled workers. Other duties are:

1. Inspecting the different jobs being performed.
2. Requesting the materials necessary for the job.
3. Presenting periodic reports of jobs completed.

Appendix 3-3. Job evaluation manual

This job evaluation manual provides a standardized method for expressing qualitative requirements in terms of a categorical scale. The factors involved are:

1. Education.
2. Experience.
3. Degree of responsibility or initiative.

For its application in evaluating the various jobs surveyed, follow these instructions: Do not be concerned about the personal characteristics of each of the individuals occupying specific positions. Concentrate rather on the characteristics required for a satisfactory compliance with the tasks inherent to these positions.

When carrying out such analysis proceed along the following stages:

First Stage: Evaluate each position separately with respect to the factors defined in this manual. Regarding each factor, consider first the definitions of the different evaluation level.

Second Stage: The evaluations must be tested for consistency after each position has been evaluated independently. This can be accomplished by comparing the evaluations for the different positions, for every factor, in order to check whether they are compatible with the characteristics (degree of difficulty, etc.) of each position.

Third Stage: Reconsider the evaluations for those positions which appear to be inconsistent when compared with all the others.

The information supplied by the firm should be utilized as much as possible following these three stages. If possible, this work should be done with the personnel manager, or a similar firm executive.

Qualitative Requirement Scales

Factor 1: Education

Education refers to the knowledge and skills developed through a learning and training program taken outside the firm or within it. In evaluating educational requirements the degree of difficulty of each position must be considered. Furthermore, the evaluation should be made in terms of the

39

education an individual must have in order to perform satisfactorily the tasks in question.

Grade 1. No education. This grade comprises all jobs for which no general or specific knowledge is required. They involve tasks so simple that they can be executed by an illiterate person (for example, janitors, sweepers).

Grade 2. Some education (1 to 2 years). This grade comprises all jobs requiring:

1. A knowledge of the four basic arithmetic operations.

2. Some proficiency in their application to the whole numbers field.

3. A knowledge of reading and writing.

These jobs should involve simple tasks for which no other ability is necessary (e.g., bricklayers, delivery boys).

Grade 3. Elementary education (3 to 4 years). This grade comprises all jobs requiring:

1. A relatively good knowledge of the four basic arithmetic operations with integers and fractions.

2. The capacity to read and write.

These jobs should involve relatively simple tasks demanding special abilities capable of being learned while performing them (e.g., assistant storekeepers, tinsmiths, plumbers).

Grade 4. Elementary education and some technical knowledge (5 to 6 years). This grade comprises all jobs requiring the abilities necessary for Grade 3, plus relatively simple technical abilities. The latter must be of the type that could be acquired in instruction and training programs of, at most, two years. The tasks involved must be of little complexity and demand only certain specific abilities (for example, electricians, machinists, invoice clerks).

Grade 5. Secondary education in a high or technical school (7 to 8 years). This grade comprises jobs requiring certain technical knowledge, like the skill to read, interpret, and prepare technical designs of operating machines and precision measuring devices. Alternatively, the knowledge of certain subjects (such as accounting and mathematics) may be required (e.g., IBM operators, lathe operators, toolsmiths).

Grade 6. Secondary and specialized education (9 to 11 years). This grade comprises jobs for which the knowledge necessary for Grade 5 is required, plus some further general or technical knowledge that can be acquired during courses or training programs of a maximum of three years (e.g., bookkeepers, project designers, specialists in electrical or mechanical maintenance).

Grade 7. Higher education (up to 17 years). This grade comprises jobs requiring the completion of secondary schooling plus some university education (e.g., engineers, accountants, architects).

Grade 8. University and specialized education (more than 17 years). This grade comprises positions requiring a university degree plus some graduate work, training, or specialization (for example, economists, statisticians, medical doctors).

Factor 2: Experience

Experience refers to the knowledge and skills learned by working. To evaluate a particular job the degree of difficulty of the tasks involved must be considered first. Then, in order to determine the requirements of particular jobs, it is necessary to appraise the experience needed to perform them satisfactorily.

Grade 1. No experience.

Grade 2. Experience of one to three months.

Grade 3. Experience of three months to one year.

Grade 4. Experience of one to three years.

Grade 5. Experience of three to five years.

Grade 6. Experience of more than five years.

Factor 3: Degree of responsibility or initiative

This factor refers to the set of personal abilities that enable an individual to analyze and compare different situations and the problems they pose, to study alternative solutions to them, and to chose the most adequate of these. It also involves the ability to establish the means and ways to make a solution functional. The evaluations have again to consider the difficulties entailed by the jobs surveyed, as well as the requirements that their satisfactory performance would entail in terms of initiative and responsibility.

Grade 1. Very simple and routine tasks. The employee must follow complete and rigid instructions or he might be under immediate supervision, not being able to make decisions without previous consultation.

Grade 2. Highly standardized tasks. The employee must follow previously established practices; he might also work under a supervisor offering frequent guidance and control. Occasionally the employee might make simple and unimportant decisions, in accordance with precedents previously sanctioned by supervisors.

Grade 3. Tasks with an average degree of standardization executed under the direction of a supervisor who allows the worker to make frequent decisions. However, the supervisor can only authorize these decisions whenever unequivocal precedents exist.

Grade 4. Tasks with little or no standardization, executed under the general guidance of a supervisor. The employee is allowed to make decisions on the methods to be used in order to attain given objectives. The decisions are frequent, but of little importance most of the time. In some cases they might imply greater responsibilities, but whenever this happens, they must strictly follow well established precedents.

Grade 5. Nonstandardized tasks executed independently. All responsibility for planning the work lies with the employee. Still, the employee follows general norms and procedures, complementing or adapting these to suit specific circumstances.

Grade 6. Difficult and complex tasks involving independent decisions affecting important activities of the firm.

Chapter 4. Interindustry wage differentials

In this chapter an attempt is made to measure in net terms the wage differentials existing among the LAFTA countries. To begin with, sector and industry are homogenized across countries, with the comparison undertaken on an industry by industry basis within the manufacturing sector. In addition, the comparisons are made for job definitions requiring the same education, experience, and responsibility. Thus the comparisons are based on uniformity of these qualitative requirements. The range of occupations covered is very similar in each industry and country. However, the comparisons are not undertaken in terms of occupations, with all of these being pooled in the statistical experiments. In chapter 6 the occupational variable will be brought into the analysis.

Thus in chapter 4 it is assumed that, within the manufacturing sector, intercountry differences in wage levels are likely to be due more to variation in job content and the qualitative requirements related to it than to variation in the composition of occupations or positions. In fact, according to some authors the contribution of occupational classification to wage differences in general, if strictly defined, is probably small, with job content being much more influential.[1] This seems to be especially true in Latin America, where workers and employees with the same qualitative characteristics appear to draw similar compensation in related occupations.[2]

This would also follow from the hedonic approach to demand theory discussed in chapter 2, which maintains that each good and service can be decomposed into a number of characteristics and that each of these is what interests the buyer. If perfectly competitive long-run equilibrium holds in a particular market, the price of each element should be the same irrespective of the good or service in which it is incorporated. Hence, goods and services with the same characteristics or elements should have the same prices even though they might appear to be of a different nature. Under disequilibrium conditions or imperfect competition, such forces can be partially,

1. See Otis Duncan, "Occupational Differences in Income," *Journal of the American Statistical Association* 56, no. 296 (December 1961).
2. For some evidence on this, see Jorge Salazar-Carrillo, "A Comparative Analysis of Government Wages and Salaries in LAFTA Countries," *Resumen del XIX ECIEL Seminar,* (Washington, D.C.: Brookings Institution, 1973).

but never totally, thwarted. That is, at any specific moment in time occupational differentials in a particular market would be mostly due to such variables as education and experience, rather than to the occupation or position. Some tests of this proposition are undertaken later.

The metallurgical, pharmaceutical, and textile industries are the ones used for the international comparisons undertaken in this chapter, for the reasons noted in chapter 3. The wages in each of these industries are compared for all countries, except Bolivia and Mexico where data for one industry is missing (the metallurgical industry in Bolivia and the pharmaceutical industry in Mexico). Wage differentials as measured in this chapter are based on all the occupations included in the survey, and not just the key positions described in appendix 2 to chapter 3. Net salary or take-home pay is the wage concept used. In the next chapter a similar set of comparisons will be presented in terms of labor cost.

Average wages by industry

The overall average hourly net wages for each of the three industries mentioned are shown in table 4-1 for every LAFTA country. Wages refer to November 1966 and were converted to U.S. dollars by using the official exchange rates.[3] A LAFTA average, which serves as the base for the wage relatives presented in the table, is also included.[4]

Some might question the use of the official exchange rates as conversion factors. However, at this point the objective is to consider money rather than real wages and thus no adjustments are made for the differing purchasing power of income in the various LAFTA countries. Later on, real wages in these industries will be compared across the LAFTA countries.

One surprising fact is immediately apparent from table 4-1: the overall LAFTA wage is similar in each of the three industries considered, even though there are significant interindustry differences within most countries. Furthermore, the textile industry, which on the basis of other studies is expected to have significantly lower relative wages, does not rank lowest.[5]

Another interesting fact emerging from table 4-1 is that the wage disparities and the rankings differ considerably by country.[6] Every industry

3. International Monetary Fund, *International Financial Statistics* (Washington, D.C., 1967). These were the exchange rates prevailing at the end of the month.

4. Both the country and the LAFTA averages used in this section are unweighted, arithmetic averages. No adjustments for differences in job content across countries or industries were made in the calculations on which table 4-1 is based.

5. See International Labour Office, "Changing Wage Structures: An International Review," *International Labour Review* 73 (March 1956), pp. 275-83.

6. These differences tend to cancel out across countries, thus leading to the close industry wage averages for the region as a whole.

Table 4-1. Money wages per hour for each LAFTA country and
relative to LAFTA average, by type of industry, November 1966[a]

Country	Textiles Absolute ($)	Textiles Relative	Pharmaceuticals Absolute ($)	Pharmaceuticals Relative	Metallurgy Absolute ($)	Metallurgy Relative
Argentina	0.72	0.86	0.61	0.73	0.72	0.78
Bolivia[b]	0.28	0.33	0.43	0.52	-	-
Brazil	0.80	0.95	0.55	0.66	0.66	0.72
Chile	0.74	0.88	0.53	0.64	0.71	0.77
Colombia	0.87	1.04	1.04	1.25	1.00	1.09
Ecuador	0.58	0.69	0.58	0.70	0.59	0.64
Mexico[b]	0.81	0.96	-	-	1.33	1.45
Paraguay	0.72	0.86	0.45	0.54	0.58	0.63
Peru	1.51	1.80	1.56	1.88	1.08	1.17
Uruguay	0.72	0.86	0.50	0.60	0.59	0.64
Venezuela	1.46	1.74	2.07	2.49	1.97	2.14
LAFTA average	0.84	1.00	0.83	1.00	0.92	1.00
Coefficient of variation	0.41		0.64		0.46	

[a] Converted into U.S. dollars by means of official exchange rates taken from International Monetary Fund, *International Financial Statistics* (Washington, D.C., 1967). The concept used is that of net wages or take-home pay and adjustment for diversity in job content across countries or industries is undertaken.

[b] No comparable data could be obtained on the metallurgical industry in Bolivia and the pharmaceutical industry in Mexico.

has the highest wages in at least one country. Table 4-2 shows these rankings by country and for LAFTA as a whole.

Taking each industry at a time, it is found that in the textile industry Peru and Venezuela have the highest wage rates and Bolivia and Ecuador the lowest, with all other countries being relatively close to the LAFTA average. A similar pattern emerges in the pharmaceutical industry, except that now Paraguay appears, instead of Ecuador, among the countries with the lowest wage rates in LAFTA. In the metallurgical industry Venezuela and Mexico show the highest wage levels, while Ecuador, Paraguay, and Uruguay have the lowest.

To be compared in real terms, wages must be converted into a common currency by means of purchasing power parity exchange rates. Real wage comparisons are especially pertinent for the study of labor migration, given that they represent an adjustment to money wages in order to reflect their real purchasing power in terms of goods and services.

Table 4-2. Ranking of hourly money wages in the three
industries by country and for LAFTA as a whole,
November 1966[a]

Country	Rank		
	1	2	3
Argentina	T	M	P
Bolivia[b]	P	T	-
Brazil	T	M	P
Chile	T	M	P
Colombia	P	M	T
Ecuador	M	TP[c]	-
Mexico[b]	M	T	-
Paraguay	T	M	P
Peru	P	T	M
Uruguay	T	M	P
Venezuela	P	M	T
LAFTA	M	T	P

[a] T = Textiles, M = Metallurgy, P = Pharmaceuticals. See table 4-1 for other details on the wage concepts used.

[b] No comparable data could be obtained on the metallurgical industry in Bolivia and the pharmaceutical industry in Mexico.

[c] The textile and pharmaceutical industries had the same average wage in Ecuador.

Purchasing power parity rates (PPP rates), which equalize the purchasing power of money in the countries involved, are now accepted as the appropriate conversion factors for most value data comparisons. The PPP rates used in this study were calculated by the Economic Commission for Latin America (ECLA) on the basis of the final prices of a common basket of consumer goods and services. Prices were collected in all Latin American countries and in the United States in 1960 and 1962. The weights used were average Latin American quantity weights. The purchasing power parities were extrapolated to the end of 1966 by using disaggregated consumer price index series.[7]

7. For further information and references on the ECLA survey and its extrapolation, see Stanley Braithwaite, "Real Income Levels in Latin America," *Review of Income and Wealth* 14 (June 1968). On PPP rates and real wage comparisons in general, see Joseph Grunwald and Jorge Salazar-Carrillo, "Economic Integration, Rates of Exchange and Price and Value Comparisons in Latin America" in *International Comparisons of Prices and Output,* ed. Don Daly (National Bureau of Economic Research, 1972); and International Labor Office, *International Comparisons of Real Wages,* (Geneva: ILO, 1965).

The wage averages for the industries examined are presented in real terms in table 4-3. In general, the conclusions derived from the money wage comparisons are altered to a large extent. First, when converted into U.S. dollars, the wages in the various LAFTA countries are much higher in real terms. This is because in terms of its command of goods and services, the dollar has a much lower purchasing power than the other LAFTA currencies. Second, because the purchasing power of wages at the end of 1966 was particularly high in Uruguay, Colombia, and Mexico relative to the other LAFTA countries, their positions in table 4-3 are significantly improved. Exactly the opposite result occurs in the case of Venezuela, Brazil, and Argentina, countries which had relatively high prices and thus relatively lower purchasing power of money in 1966. Finally, in each of the three industries the intercountry dispersion is much lower when real rather than money wages are considered (see coefficients of variation in tables 4-1 and 4-3).

Table 4-3. Real wages per hour for each LAFTA country and relative to LAFTA average, by type of industry, November 1966[a]

Country	Textiles		Pharmaceuticals		Metallurgy	
	Absolute ($)	Relative	Absolute ($)	Relative	Absolute ($)	Relative
Argentina	0.94	0.76	0.79	0.68	0.93	0.73
Bolivia[b]	0.43	0.35	0.63	0.54	-	-
Brazil	0.89	0.72	0.62	0.53	0.74	0.58
Chile	1.09	0.89	0.77	0.66	1.04	0.81
Colombia	1.54	1.25	1.84	1.57	1.77	1.38
Ecuador	0.96	0.78	0.96	0.82	0.97	0.76
Mexico[b]	1.38	1.12	-	-	2.27	1.77
Paraguay	1.16	0.94	0.73	0.62	0.94	0.73
Peru	1.98	1.61	2.05	1.75	1.42	1.11
Uruguay	1.45	1.18	1.00	0.85	1.18	0.92
Venezuela	1.66	1.35	2.34	2.00	2.24	1.75
LAFTA average	1.23	1.00	1.17	1.00	1.28	1.00
Coefficient of variation	0.33		0.52		0.39	

[a] Converted into U.S. dollars by means of unpublished purchasing power parity rates for November 1966, provided by the Economic Comission for Latin America (ECLA). The figures correspond to net wages or take-home pay and no adjustment for diversity in job content across countries or industries is undertaken.

[b] No comparable data could be obtained on the metallurgical industry in Bolivia and the pharmaceutical industry in Mexico.

Wage comparisons for homogeneous job contents by industry

The variation in wages resulting from the impact of the qualitative variables defining job content seems to be greater than those arising out of industry or employment. Such an indication is provided by the fact that interskill differences have generally been found to be wider than interindustry differentials, especially if the latter are based on a comparable job content.[8] This is why the insistence on homogeneous qualitative requirements is crucial for precise intercountry comparisons. The high wages in Mexico, for instance, may be partially due to the fact that its workers are better trained and more experienced. Only if wages are adjusted to take such factors into account would Mexican wages be comparable to those of other LAFTA countries.

In order to homogenize job content and qualitative requirements across countries, the metholology described in chapter 2 was applied and regressions were run at the industry level, relating the qualitative and country variables to wages. Of the three wage variants used in the survey—minimum, average, and maximum salaries—the qualitative requirements were related only to the first because minimum wages were handled with greater care in the survey and kept more homogeneous across countries.

The textile industry

The first industry to be analyzed in this fashion is the textile industry. Its regression equation is:

$$\begin{aligned}
\text{Log Wage} =\ & 0.66138 + \underset{(0.07260)}{0.12642} \text{ Arg} - \underset{(0.06466)}{0.16847} \text{ Bol} - \underset{(0.09335)}{0.58101} \text{ Ecu} \\
& + \underset{(0.05939)}{0.31410} \text{ Uru} + \underset{(0.11640)}{0.54795} \text{ Mex} + \underset{(0.00681)}{0.08183} \text{ Edu} - \underset{(0.01534)}{0.04393} \text{ Eduarg} \\
& - \underset{(0.02143)}{0.11092} \text{ Edubra} + \underset{(0.01654)}{0.05289} \text{ Eduecu} - \underset{(0.01353)}{0.05321} \text{ Eduuru} - \underset{(0.01906)}{0.06626} \text{ Edumex} \\
& + \underset{(0.00535)}{0.02823} \text{ Exp} + \underset{(0.02273)}{0.04225} \text{ Expbra} + \underset{(0.00574)}{0.02109} \text{ Expper} + \underset{(0.00643)}{0.07379} \text{ Resp} \\
& - \underset{(0.01861)}{0.09473} \text{ Respbol} + \underset{(0.02492)}{0.07326} \text{ Respbra} - \underset{(0.02756)}{0.04991} \text{ Respmex.}
\end{aligned}$$

The labeling in this equation has purposely been made explicit. The variables with just country names are the intercept dummies. The variables

8. On this point, see Belton M. Fleisher, *Labor Economics: Theory and Evidence*, (Englewood Cliffs, N.J.: Prentice-Hall, 1970), p. 212; and E. M. Hugh-Jones, ed., *Wage-Structure in Theory and Practice,* (Amsterdam: North-Holland, 1966), pp. 93–143 and various chapters on specific countries.

measuring the basic effect of the independent variables over wages are clearly labeled without any country abbreviation. For example, the overall or basic coefficient for education is labeled *Edu*. On the other hand, the slope dummies measuring the interaction between countries and qualitative variables have a country ending (e.g., *Eduarg* for education in Argentina). The standard errors of these coefficients appear in parentheses under them, with only significant coefficients (at the 0.10 level) retained in the final equation.

By introducing the qualitative factors mentioned, together with the country variables, the degree of explanation of the wages variation obtained is quite satisfactory for a cross-section ($R^2 = 0.64$) adjusted for degrees of freedom.[9]

The basic coefficients have the expected signs, indicating a positive relationship between wages and education, experience, and degree of responsibility or initiative.

At the general equation level there are no restrictions that can be placed on the signs of the dummy variables as a result of theoretical expectations. However, as shown below, restrictions can be placed on the signs of the coefficients in country equations derived from the general equation. For the textile industry, country equations are derived by retaining the country dummies that are significant and adding their coefficients to the basic ones. For example, examine the following equation corresponding to Argentina:

$$\text{Log Wage} = [0.66138 + (0.12642)] + [0.08183 + (-0.04393)] \text{ Edu} + 0.02823 \text{ Exp} + 0.07379 \text{ Resp.}$$

In this equation whenever a dummy variable is included, its coefficient is enclosed in parenthesis and is added to the basic coefficient. Thus, the country coefficient for education in Argentina is 0.03790, which results from adding to the basic coefficient (0.08183) the slope dummy coefficient for education in Argentina (-0.04393).

With two exceptions the signs of the statistically significant country coefficients comply with theoretical expectations. The exceptions are the coefficient for education in Brazil and the coefficient for degree of responsibility in Bolivia which appear with negative signs. As explained in chapter 2, in such cases it was decided to keep the coefficients in the equations, even though they did not agree with theoretical expectations.

As noted in the previous section, the homogenization of job content across countries is an essential step for the measurement of intercountry wage differentials in net terms. This can be accomplished by ascertaining

9. This flexible pooling regression was run on a sample of 913 observations.

Table 4-4. Estimated real wages per hour in the textile industry
for each LAFTA country, November 1966[a]

Country	1st Quartile			2nd Quartile			3rd Quartile		
	Absolute ($)	Relative (%)	Rank	Absolute ($)	Relative (%)	Rank	Absolute ($)	Relative (%)	Rank
Argentina	0.56	97	(8)	0.77	94	(8)	1.06	91	(8)
Bolivia	0.34	59	(9)	0.42	51	(11)	0.51	44	(11)
Brazil	0.32	55	(10)	0.50	61	(9)	0.77	66	(10)
Chile	0.63	109	(4)	0.96	117	(3)	1.46	126	(2)
Colombia	0.63	109	(4)	0.96	117	(3)	1.46	126	(2)
Ecuador	0.27	47	(11)	0.46	56	(10)	0.79	68	(9)
Mexico	1.07	184	(1)	1.25	152	(1)	1.46	126	(2)
Paraguay	0.63	109	(4)	0.96	117	(3)	1.46	126	(2)
Peru	0.69	119	(3)	1.10	134	(2)	1.77	153	(1)
Uruguay	0.79	136	(2)	1.07	107	(7)	1.44	124	(7)
Venezuela	0.63	109	(4)	0.96	117	(3)	1.46	126	(2)
LAFTA average	0.58	100		0.82	100		1.16	100	
Coefficient of variation	0.3663			0.3122			0.3028		

Kendall coefficient of concordance = 0.892 at the 0.01 level of significance.

[a] Converted into dollars by using unpublished purchasing power parity rates provided by the Economic Commission for Latin America for November 1966. The figures correspond to net wages or take-home pay, and are adjusted for diversity of job content across countries.

quartile values of the qualitative requirements from the sample information as explained in the methodological chapters, and keeping them fixed across countries. Wage differentials were then calculated by computing the hypothetical wages corresponding to these job contents in each country using the equation for that industry. For the textile industry, the values of the three qualitative variables at the quartile locations are:[10]

	Education	*Experience*	*Responsibility*
1st quartile	4	2	1
2nd quartile	5	3	2
3rd quartile	6	4	3

The hourly wages for the different LAFTA countries corresponding to these quartile values are presented in table 4-4 in terms of U.S. dollars. They have been converted by means of purchasing power parity rates and thus are in real terms. Wage relatives are also shown, with the LAFTA average as the base.

One thing apparent from tables 4-3 and 4-4 is that after the homogenization of qualitative requirements, the wage differentials among LAFTA countries change substantially. Second, there is good agreement in the wage differentials, and among the countries' rankings at different levels of the qualitative variables (quartiles), as shown by the Kendall coefficient of concordance. Still, it is interesting to note that wage dispersion becomes progressively lower at higher levels of the qualitative variables (see coefficients of variation). Thus the effect of the country slope dummies over the wage comparison seems to be significant, if not overwhelming, which in turn means that the implicit prices of education, experience, and responsibility vary across countries.

The absolute wage levels corresponding to the different quartiles, even in real or purchasing power terms (which raises them in comparisons with the United States), are quite low contrasted with U.S. minimum wages. Of the three quartiles, the first one would be the best approximation to the job content of minimum wage workers in the United States. At the first quartile Mexico is the only country with real wage levels close to the U.S. minimum, which was $1.25 an hour at the end of 1966.

Finally, the interskill differentials, denoted by a comparison of the wages at the various quartiles, appear to differ substantially on a country by country basis. The relation of third quartile to first quartile wages is less

10. For a description of what each of these levels represent in terms of actual education, experience, and responsibility, see chapter 3, appendix 3.

than 1.5 in Mexico and close to 3.0 in the case of Ecuador, with most countries having ratios well over 2.0. This suggests significantly different rewards to higher skills throughout LAFTA, signaling that their relative scarcities or the functioning of the labor markets for the diverse skills in question, vary widely across LAFTA countries.

The intercountry net wage differentials for the industry can be combined into a single scale by assigning weights to each quartile. To derive such weights, the relative frequency of each quartile set of qualitative values in the overall textile industry sample is determined. The quartile weights derived from such relative frequencies are:

1st quartile	0.22
2nd quartile (median)	0.52
3rd quartile	0.26

The index used to combine the three quartiles is a geometric wage relative formulation, with the LAFTA weights just described. The geometric mean has a definite advantage in that, compared with the arithmetic average, it is less affected by extreme values. With this index it is percentage deviations rather than absolute deviations that are revelant. It can be expressed as:

$$\Pi = \sum_{x=1}^{3} \left(\frac{W_{ax}}{W_{bx}} \right) \times N_{ox}$$

where:

W_{ax} = wage in a certain country for a particular quartile.
W_{bx} = average LAFTA wage for a particular quartile.
N_{ox} = relative number of workers in LAFTA having the sets of qualitative values corresponding to each quartile.
x = quartiles (3).
a = countries (11).

On the basis of the quartile wages and weights discussed previously, an overall index for the textile industry in the LAFTA region is presented in table 4-5. After account is taken of influence of job content on wage levels, Mexico, followed by Peru, appears to have the highest wages in the textile industry, substantially above the average LAFTA levels. Bolivia, Ecuador, and Brazil have the lowest levels of wages, also quite apart from the LAFTA average. The rest of the countries have very similar wage levels. In fact,

Table 4-5. Index of real wages in the textile industry for
LAFTA countries, November 1966
(LAFTA average = 100)

Country	Index	Rank
Argentina	94	(8)
Bolivia	51	(11)
Brazil	61	(9)
Chile	117	(3)
Colombia	117	(3)
Ecuador	57	(10)
Mexico	151	(1)
Paraguay	117	(3)
Peru	135	(2)
Uruguay	117	(3)
Venezuela	117	(3)
Coefficient of Variation = 0.3063		

the wages of Chile, Paraguay, Colombia, Uruguay, and Venezuela were not significantly different from each other after normalization. Finally, it should be noted that intercountry wage dispersion decreased after wages were normalized (see coefficient of variation in tables 4-3 and 4-6).

It is interesting to note that Bolivian wages are raised considerably after adjusting for the effect of varying qualitative requirements. This means that the very low Bolivian wages before normalization were due to the relatively low levels of education, experience, and degree of responsibility required from Bolivian workers by the firms. The same thing occurs in the cases of Chile and Mexico, although the resulting upward wage adjustments are not as acute.

On the other hand, just the opposite phenomenon affects the positions of Argentina, Venezuela, and principally Ecuador after wages were normalized. The high wages in these countries appeared to have been accompanied by relatively higher values of qualitative factors. Thus, as the latter were homogenized across countries the wages of these countries became correspondingly lower.

The pharmaceutical industry

The flexible pooling equation corresponding to the pharmaceutical industry follows, with the specifications and variables being like those in the textile industry equation.

Table 4-6. Estimated real wages per hour in the pharmaceutical industry for each LAFTA country, November 1966[a]

Country	1st Quartile			2nd Quartile			3rd Quartile		
	Absolute ($)	Relative (%)	Rank	Absolute ($)	Relative (%)	Rank	Absolute ($)	Relative (%)	Rank
Argentina	0.68	110	(3)	0.77	92	(6)	0.86	74	(8)
Bolivia	0.62	100	(5)	0.78	93	(4)	0.98	84	(5)
Brazil	0.39	63	(9)	0.58	69	(10)	0.87	75	(7)
Chile	0.62	100	(5)	0.78	93	(4)	0.98	84	(5)
Colombia	0.75	121	(2)	1.13	135	(2)	1.71	147	(2)
Ecuador	0.54	87	(7)	0.66	79	(8)	0.81	70	(9)
Mexico	-	-	-	-	-	-	-	-	-
Paraguay	0.50	81	(8)	0.62	74	(9)	0.76	66	(10)
Peru	0.35	56	(10)	0.68	81	(7)	1.30	112	(3)
Uruguay	0.63	102	(4)	0.79	94	(3)	1.00	86	(4)
Venezuela	1.07	173	(1)	1.59	189	(1)	2.35	202	(1)
LAFTA average	0.62	100		0.84	100		1.16	100	
Coefficient of variation	0.3125			0.3448			0.4113		

Kendall coefficient of concordance = 0.8048 at the 0.01 level of significance.

[a] Converted into U.S. dollars by using the unpublished purchasing power parities calculated by the Economic Commission for Latin America for November 1966. The figures correspond to net wages or take-home pay, and are adjusted for diversity of job content across countries. There was strong resistance from the Mexican pharmaceutical industry to collaborate in the survey. In the end, this industry did not provide comparable data in time to be included in the intercountry comparisons.

Log Wage = − 0.67176 + 0.37423 Arg − 0.22004 Bra + 0.49010 Ecu
                    (0.08097)   (0.08946)   (0.15032)
+ 0.30182 Ven − 0.32371 Peru + 0.36228 Uru + 0.11586 Edu
   (0.06200)   (0.03257)   (0.06282)   (0.00916)
− 0.09466 Eduarg − 0.17805 Eduecu − 0.04616 Eduven − 0.05120 Eduper
   (0.01834)   (0.03400)   (0.01574)   (0.02037)
− 0.11896 Eduuru + 0.01737 Exp − 0.06149 Expbra − 0.08776 Exppar
   (0.01835)   (0.00584)   (0.02646)   (0.01252)
+ 0.04755 Expper + 0.04670 Resp − 0.03481 Resparg − 0.08006 Respbol
   (0.02377)   (0.00927)   (0.01907)   (0.01367)
+ 0.05698 Respbra − 0.07989 Respchi + 0.08475 Respecu
   (0.02234)   (0.00982)   (0.02767)
+ 0.03801 Respven + 0.10757 Respper + 0.03916 Respuru.
   (0.01627)   (0.02511)   (0.01886)

The degree of explanation obtained in this equation was quite high ($\bar{R}^2 =$ 0.69, adjusted for degrees of freedom), even better than in the case of textiles. The standard errors are shown in parentheses beneath the respective coefficients with only significant coefficients (at the 0.10 level) retained in the final equation. As can be seen, the signs of all the basic coefficients are expected ones.[11]

The country equations derived from this general equation are the ones used for the calculation of the normalization wages for each nation. The three sets of quartile values for the qualitative variables, as determined by the sample frequencies, are specified below.

	Education	Experience	Responsibility
1st quartile	4	2	1
2nd quartile	5	3	2
3rd quartile	6	4	3

In table 4-6 the real wages associated with these quartiles, as well as the wages relative to the LAFTA average as a base, are presented. Noticeably, the wage levels at the qualitative values corresponding to the third quartile are spread wider than in the other quartiles, which is exactly the opposite of what occurred in the textile industry (compare coefficients of variation in tables 4-4 and 4-6). As previously, the rankings and the wage differences change as the qualitative requirements vary across quartiles. Argentina's wages, for example, which are 10% above the LAFTA average in the first quartile, are 26% below it in the third quartile, possibly reflecting a relatively more ample supply of workers with higher skills. This is due to the

11. There are 845 observations in the pharmaceutical industry.

effects of the country slope dummies, which signal that the rewards for higher skills are unequal among countries. Yet, although there is variation, the rankings of wage relatives are basically consistent across quartiles (see Kendall's coefficient of concordance).

If the wage relatives by quartile are examined for each LAFTA country, it is seen that they either rise or decline consistently from the first to the third quartile. A closer look makes evident that there is substantial diversity in interskill differentials within the region. The narrowest range is shown by Argentina whose wage relatives decline sharply in moving from the first to the third quartile, the ratio of third to first quartile wages being 1.3. Peru represents an opposite extreme, with a relative interquartile range of 3.7, and a continually improving comparative standing (the range for the LAFTA wage averages is slightly below 2.0). These ratios would again indicate the relative scarcities of various types of personnel in the different countries and/or differences in the way in which the labor markets for diverse skills operate.

Finally, if the wages for the first quartile are compared to the U.S. minimum wages, it is apparent that even though the former are in real terms, their level is much lower. In this industry, only Venezuela has real wages of over one dollar an hour at the skill levels characterizing the first quartile.

To obtain an overall index of the wage differentials the quartiles are weighted according to the frequency of each of the three combinations of qualitative factors in the LAFTA sample: 0.13, 0.45, and 0.42 for the first, second, and third quartiles respectively.

The results in table 4-7 show that Venezuela ranks at the top of the list in the pharmaceutical industry, with Colombia following. On the other hand, Brazil and Paraguay are at the other extreme. It is important to note that, again, the rest of the country index values are quite close together. In fact, the only substantial real wage differences in the pharmaceutical industry are those which appear to set Venezuela and Colombia apart from the rest of the LAFTA countries.

Comparing the results in table 4-3 with those just presented, it appears that the ranking has altered considerably after normalization. The relative wage levels of Colombia and especially Peru, for example, have decreased considerably after taking job content into account, indicating that their wages were relatively higher on account of more demanding qualitative requirements on the part of employers. The opposite occurs in the cases of Bolivia and Chile, whose relative position improves substantially after the homogenization of job content. Finally, it should be noted that wage dispersion diminishes significantly after wages have been normalized, as was

Table 4-7. Index of real wages in the pharmaceutical
industry for LAFTA countries, November 1966
(LAFTA average = 100)

Country	Index	Rank
Argentina	86	(7)
Bolivia	90	(4)
Brazil	71	(9)
Chile	90	(4)
Colombia	138	(2)
Ecuador	76	(8)
Mexico	-	-
Paraguay	71	(9)
Peru	88	(6)
Uruguay	92	(3)
Venezuela	192	(1)
Coefficient of Variation = 0.3594		

seen to be the case in the textile industry (see coefficients of variation in tables 4-3 and 4-7).

The metallurgical industry

The resulting flexible pooling equation for the metallurgical industry is:

Log Wage = −0.72227 + 0.39765 Arg + 0.15792 Bra − 0.13780 Chi
(0.09058)   (0.08870)   (0.02914)

− 0.61589 Ecu − 0.16975 Par + 0.28885 Ven − 0.32610 Per
(0.07255)   (0.05838)   (0.08522)   (0.04620)

+ 0.27370 Uru + 0.89240 Mex + 0.10555 Edu − 0.07466 Eduarg
(0.08326)   (0.07493)   (0.00789)   (0.01581)

− 0.04125 Eduven − 0.07325 Eduuru − 0.05457 Edumex + 0.04202 Exp
(0.01705)   (0.01831)   (0.01645)   (0.00688)

− 0.04796 Exppar − 0.12026 Expbra − 0.04001 Expmex + 0.05324 Resp
(0.01415)   (0.02663)   (0.01866)   (0.00723)

+ 0.08242 Respecu + 0.06131 Respper − 0.06134 Respmex.
(0.08242)   (0.01344)   (0.02024)

The coefficient of determination $(\bar{R}^2)$ is 0.65 after adjustment for degrees of freedom, which is quite satisfactory for a cross-section. The estimating equation for this industry was based on a sample of 847 observations. The coefficients of the general equation are well behaved, having the expected signs and being significant at the 0.10 level. However, this is not

Table 4-8. Estimated real wages per hour in the metallurgical industry for each LAFTA country, November 1966[a]

Country	1st Quartile Absolute ($)	1st Quartile Relative (%)	1st Quartile Rank	2nd Quartile Absolute ($)	2nd Quartile Relative (%)	2nd Quartile Rank	3rd Quartile Absolute ($)	3rd Quartile Relative (%)	3rd Quartile Rank
Argentina	0.80	127	(2)	1.08	129	(3)	1.63	124	(3)
Bolivia	-	-	-	-	-	-	-	-	-
Brazil	0.45	71	(6)	0.54	64	(7)	0.73	56	(9)
Chile	0.39	62	(7)	0.62	74	(6)	1.12	85	(7)
Colombia	0.54	86	(5)	0.86	102	(4)	1.54	118	(4)
Ecuador	0.16	25	(10)	0.30	36	(10)	0.79	60	(8)
Mexico	1.95	310	(1)	2.11	251	(1)	2.24	171	(1)
Paraguay	0.29	46	(8)	0.42	50	(9)	0.67	51	(10)
Peru	0.29	46	(8)	0.54	64	(7)	1.28	98	(5)
Uruguay	0.61	97	(4)	0.82	98	(5)	1.24	95	(6)
Venezuela	0.79	125	(3)	1.14	136	(2)	1.86	142	(2)
LAFTA average	0.63	100		0.84	100		1.31	100	
Coefficient of variation	0.7727			0.5880			0.3724		

Kendall coefficient of concordance = 0.9208 at the 0.01 level of significance.

[a]The conversion rates used are unpublished purchasing power parity rates provided by the Economic Commission for Latin America, corresponding to November 1966. The figures correspond to net wages or take-home pay, and are adjusted for diversity of job content across countries. Bolivia was not included because the metallurgical industry is almost nonexistent in that country.

the case with some of the coefficients of the derived country equations; those of responsibility in Mexico and experience in Brazil have negative signs.

The values of the independent variables used to normalize the qualitative requirements in this industry are:

	Education	Experience	Responsibility
1st quartile	3	2	1
2nd quartile (median)	4	3	2
3rd quartile	5	4	4

In table 4-8 the absolute and relative wage levels in real terms are presented, and the countries ranked accordingly. An examination of the table shows that the real wage levels in the metallurgical industry are above those in the textile and pharmaceutical industries, although the differences are rather small after the qualitative requirements have been normalized. This is the case even though the quartile requirements for education are lower in the metallurgical industry.[12]

The rankings vary from quartile to quartile; however, a clear pattern of high and low wage countries appears. Mexican wages are quite high, even in the lowest quartile. An hourly wage of $1.95, which was above minimum wages in the United States for the corresponding time period, has to be explained not only in terms of proximity to the United States but also as a result of high labor productivity in the industry. The wages in the other countries are well below U.S. minimum wages at the first quartile values of the qualitative variables, with Venezuela being the country with the second highest wage level ($0.79 an hour). In general, first quartile wages again appear to be substantially below those corresponding to comparable jobs in the United States, reflecting a wide disparity in living standards. Considering the wages at each quartile separately, and then relating them to each other, interesting facts emerge. The dispersion in wages is greatest in the first quartile in this industry, and smallest in the third quartile (as shown by the respective coefficients of variation). The wage relatives of various countries, under the effect of slope dummies, vary substantially across quartiles, with either an upward or downward pattern being evident. Again, interskill wage differentials are quite diverse. The relative interquartile range is 1.2 in the case of Mexico, whose wage relatives narrow consistently from the first to the third quartile. On the other hand, for Peru and Ecuador whose wage relatives widen, the ratio is well above 4.0.

Finally, when quartiles are combined into an overall index, it is found

12. However, the third quartile value for responsibility in the metallurgical industry is one level higher than in the other two industries.

Table 4-9. Index of real wages in the metallurgical
industry for LAFTA countries, November 1966
(LAFTA average = 100)

Country	Index	Rank
Argentina	127	(3)
Bolivia	-	-
Brazil	62	(8)
Chile	76	(6)
Colombia	108	(4)
Ecuador	41	(10)
Mexico	227	(1)
Paraguay	50	(9)
Peru	71	(7)
Uruguay	97	(5)
Venezuela	136	(2)
Coefficient of Variation = 0.5228		

that Mexico and Venezuela have much higher wages, and Ecuador and
Paraguay much lower ones, than the rest of LAFTA (see table 4-9).[13]

The rest of the countries could be sub-classified in two groups: Brazil,
Chile, and Peru in one; and Uruguay, Colombia, and Argentina in the
other. The first group has wage levels which are about 30% below the
LAFTA average, while those in the second group are approximately equal to
that average.

Comparing these results with the real wage relatives before adjustment
for varying job content (see table 4-3), important changes are evident. The
real wages of Mexico and Argentina are considerably raised after the qualitative requirements are homogenized. On the other hand, many countries
experience substantial reductions in their real wages after normalization,
predominantly Peru and Ecuador. As a result, the rankings also change
significantly.

Finally, the dispersion in the wage relatives in this industry is increased
after wages have been adjusted to correspond to a homogeneous job content (see coefficient of variation in tables 4-3 and 4-9). This stands in contrast with the previous two industries, in which the net wage differentials

13. The weights used in the computation of the index are:

1st quartile	0.13
2nd quartile	0.54
3rd quartile	0.33

It is interesting to note that these quartile weights vary substantially by industry.

were less dispersed than the gross wage differentials. This illustrates the fact that, if wage differentials are not calculated as much as possible in net terms, it probably is impossible to be certain even of the direction of the bias in their estimation. Measured in gross terms, wage differences may turn out to be wider or narrower than the true ones, although it would be expected that they would generally be wider.

In the case of the metallurgical industry, the increased dispersion after adjustment comes about as a result of the relationship between a country's wages and the qualitative requirements for the jobs considered. High wage levels may correspond to high qualitative requirements and low wages to low qualitative requirements. After normalization these wages are adjusted downwards and upwards respectively and dispersion tends to diminish. However, it may turn out that high wages do not correlate with high qualitative requirements (as in the cases of Argentina and Mexico); low wages may go hand in hand with relatively high requirements (as in Peru and Ecuador). Under such circumstances dispersion may increase.

Intercountry wage differences in the overall industrial sample

Although the results for each of the industries covered are not that different (especially considering their country rankings), the diversity found is still significant. To express net wage differentials for the various industries considered in a less ambiguous fashion, a weighted index combining previous results is constructed. For this purpose a weighted geometric mean formulation appears to be the most appropriate. There are several likely choices as weights for the three industries involved. The most reasonable appears to be either employment or gross product in each industry. An industry characterized by more capital intensive technology, for example, might provide less employment; yet, higher wage rates could compensate for this and the total wage bill may in the end be larger. Thus, gross industrial product seems to be the best proxy for an industry's wage bill that is generally unavailable.

The weights used in the overall index were first calculated on a country by country basis and then aggregated to correspond to the whole of LAFTA. Such a procedure opens the possibility of comparing wages on a binary basis as well as in terms of smaller subgroupings, like the Andean Group. However, in the comparisons only the geometric mean of all LAFTA country weights were used. The real wage indices for the three industries combined are presented in table 4-10, with the country rankings also shown.

It appears that when the three industries are combined, the resulting overall real wage levels can be divided into three groupings. First, Mexico, Venezuela, and Colombia appear to be the countries with the highest wage levels. There seems to be a large gap separating these countries, especially the first two, from the second group comprising Peru, Uruguay, Chile, Argentina, and Paraguay. Then, there is another break in the continuum, as the countries with lowest wages in real terms follow: Brazil, Bolivia, and finally Ecuador.

The position of Mexico as the leading country in terms of real take-home pay can be explained partly by its relatively low level of consumer prices. However, two other important factors that raise wages have to be mentioned. One is the proximity to the United States, a partial escape valve for the Mexican labor force, which exercises an upward pressure on wages. The other is the success of government-sponsored unionism, combined with probably the most up-to-date technology within LAFTA.

Another country whose position is somewhat startling is Brazil. Here the reverse happens, with a high price level for consumer goods and services being a major cause of a low level of real wages. Another element that undoubtedly contributes to the Brazilian position is its weak unionism. Even in money terms (see the appendix to chapter 5) the standing of Brazil is only above those of the four poorest countries in LAFTA (Paraguay, Uruguay, Bolivia, and Ecuador).[14] Finally, at the end of 1966 Brazil was suffering a severe recession which appears to have made matters worse for the workers.

The positions of Bolivia, Ecuador, and Paraguay, on the lower rungs of the wage ladder, correspond with their levels of development. No other surprises are evident in the standings except for Argentina's placement slightly below the LAFTA average. One explanation is that Argentina's generally high wage level does not hold for the particular combinations of qualitative requirements, or job contents, considered in this study. This would be due to the relatively ample supply of such skills in Argentina, and would be reflected in its generally lower interskill differentials.[15]

Furthermore, Argentina is a case where the purchasing power parity

14. Many other studies have confirmed Brazil's low position in terms of take-home pay expressed in money terms. See Haydee Castillo and Manuel Rodríguez Trujillo, *El Costo de la Mano de Obra en Venezuela* (Caracas: Fundación Eugenio Mendoza, 1965), which rates Brazil below Venezuela, Argentina, Mexico, and Colombia in terms of money wages. Also, see International Labor Organization, *Yearbook of Labor Statistics* (Geneva: ILO, 1968), whose overall industry wages after conversion by means of purchasing power parity rates would place Brazil below Venezuela, Colombia, Peru, and Ecuador. An article in the *New York Times,* January 25, 1971, shows Brazil as the lowest of nine LAFTA countries; however, in this case the Brazilian figure is for an earlier year.

15. On this point see John R. Eriksson, "Wage Structures and Economic Development in Selected Latin American Countries, A Comparative Analysis" (Ph.D. diss., University of California, Berkeley, 1966) pp. 169–77.

apparently has a great influence on the standings. Argentina's position in terms of money wages is close to that of Peru and above those of Chile and Uruguay (see the appendix to chapter 5). When the comparison shifts to real wages, it is below these three countries. This *may* be due to an underestimation of the purchasing power of the Argentina peso vis-à-vis the countries mentioned. It would appear reasonable to suspect that real wages in the modern manufacturing sector in Argentina would at least be similar to those of Peru, Uruguay, and Chile in table 4-10.

Another unexpected finding is that after normalization, real wages in Paraguay are only a bit below those of Argentina and Chile. This can be partly explained by the openness of the Paraguayan economy as well as its low consumer prices. But again, a crucial factor may be that, in contrast to those of Argentina, Paraguayan wage levels indicate a high payoff to the type of skills considered in the study. Thus, Paraguayan wages would be low when qualitative requirements are modest but when job content becomes more demanding, they would rise substantially.

Adjustments for size of firm effects

One reputedly important variable not yet considered in the measurement of the intercountry wage differentials is the size of the firm. The size of a firm

Table 4-10. Index of real wages in the overall industrial sample for LAFTA countries, November 1966[a]
(LAFTA average = 100)

Country	Index	Rank
Argentina	94	(7)
Bolivia	64	(10)
Brazil	65	(9)
Chile	101	(6)
Colombia	125	(3)
Ecuador	61	(11)
Mexico	164	(1)
Paraguay	89	(8)
Peru	107	(4)
Uruguay	105	(5)
Venezuela	143	(2)
Coefficient of Variation = 0.3077		

[a]This index is the result of combining and aggregating the textile, metallurgy, and pharmaceutical industries. Imputations were made for the missing industries in Mexico and Bolivia.

is usually correlated with both its overall productivity and the type of market structure in which it operates. In turn, productivity and market structure seem to influence profit rates and wages.[16] Thus, as wages are compared across countries, it would be quite useful to establish whether the differences are related to size of the firm, and thus indirectly to productivity and market structure. If so, the wages corresponding to the same job content in a particular industry may be higher in larger firms. As the size of firms varies across countries (probably due to varying industrial development), it might be pertinent to adjust for the effects of the size of a firm in order to obtain the closest approximation possible to the net intercountry wage differentials.[17]

The same methodology and procedures used in adjusting the homogeneous sets of qualitative requirements, considered in detail in chapters 2 and 3, are also applicable to the size of the firm adjustments, with general flexible pooling equations fitted to wage survey data for the various industries. The variables remain the same except that a size of firm variable (determined by the total number of workers in each firm) is included.

Before the adjustment for size of firm is undertaken, a note of warning is warranted. As shall be documented here, these adjustments produced some awkward results. Given that the variance of size of firm within each industry was much smaller than those of the qualitative variables, and that some of the estimated wages resulting from the inclusion of this variable in the wage equations were dubious, the wage comparisons presented previously are more reliable and should be considered the valid ones.[18] Yet, adding some comments on the intercountry wage comparisons after the influences of size of firm has been neutralized would appear to be useful. First, it permits a more careful consideration of what the size of firm adjustment really means, especially in terms of the apparent oddities encountered. Second, it allows a comparison of the results both including and excluding the effect of this variable. Third, some readers might prefer to use the results that include size of firm adjustment.

16. This has been repeatedly found by researchers in the past, particularly in Latin America because of the relatively small size of its markets. See Albert Rees, *New Measures of Wage-Earner Compensation in Manufacturing,* (Cambridge, Mass: National Bureau of Economy Research, 1960); Melvin W. Reder, *Labor in a Growing Economy* (New York: Wiley, 1958); M.C. Flaming, "Interfirm Differences in Productivity and their Relation to Occupational Structure and Size of Firm," *The Manchester School of Economics and Social Studies* 38 (September 1970).

17. One problem that may be created by adding an additional variable is that it may affect the behavior of the others, due to possible interaction effects.

18. Each firm provides only one observation on size, while each contributes many observations on the qualitative variables.

The multiple coefficients of determination (R^2), after adjustment for size of firm, increase slightly (about 1%) in the various industry equations. The total number of significant explanatory variables entering the final equation also rises. The coefficient of size of firm was significant in many cases, but not always positive as would be expected.[19] The quartile values for size of firm range from 111 to 1103 workers in the three industries. After deriving the specific country equations from the general ones, the wages corresponding to each quartile set of qualitative variables, including firm size, can be calculated. In general, the absolute wages change significantly after size of firm is normalized. This is particularly the case with the wages in Bolivia and Brazil. However, the absolute wages still remain well below those of comparable positions in the United States. The dispersion of wages across quartiles is also affected by the introduction of size of firm.

Of all the changes, the most surprising is the relatively high wages of Bolivia's pharmaceutical industry, after the adjustment for size is performed. This can be partly explained in terms of the paucity of the data in Bolivia, combined with the fact that the average size of the firm is relatively small. Thus, the hypothetical wage increases calculated for large sizes may constitute improperly founded extrapolations.

Nevertheless, as the size of firms increases, wage relations vary as a consequence of the introduction of more advanced techniques, improved organization, overall mechanization, modern management, greater control of the marketplace, etc. Thus, the comparatively low wage rates paid by firms at the lower fringes of the modern sector may be erased as the firms grow. This is an alternative explanation of high wages found for Bolivia in some of the industries sampled, after the size of firm adjustment.[20]

The case of Brazil was also quite odd in the metallurgical industry comparison. Even though Brazilian wages were not as conspicuously high as those of Bolivia, they still provoke certain doubts. This is especially true because, contrary to theoretical expectations, the size of the firm coefficient in the derived Brazilian equation for that industry is negative. This can be explained in terms of the statistical factors discussed in chapters 2 and 3, particularly the intercorrelation among the independent variables. Apart from the sign of the coefficient, the unexpectedly high wages in Brazil after the size of the firm adjustment could result from misspecifica-

19. As the size of the firm is generally directly related to overall productivity and more concentrated market structure, it would be reasonable to expect big firms to pay higher wages and vice versa.

20. A similar situation affected the wages of Ecuador. Both these countries have firms of relatively small size, and their workers would probably be paid more if they were employed in large ones.

tion of the form of the estimating equation for Brazil, or from the relatively small number of observations covering a limited range of the overall size of firm variation.

Operationally, two factors seem to account for the high relative wages estimated for Brazil's metallurgical industry: the negative sign of the size of firm coefficient, and the large size of the firms when compared to those of most other LAFTA countries. The negative coefficient inflates the calculated level of wages as the size of the firm diminishes. However, since it is not clear to what extent the results reflect reality, it is not certain that the wage levels found would hold for smaller firms in the modern metallurgical industry in Brazil.

Before ending this chapter, an overall wage comparison for the three manufacturing activities covered here is presented, after adjusting for the effects of size of firm. For this purpose an index combining the wage indices estimated for the textile, pharmaceutical, and metallurgical industries is constructed. This is done by using the same procedures previously explained. The weighting of the various industry indices, while adjusting for the fact that Mexico and Bolivia were each included in only two of these, results in the aggregated index of wage differentials and corresponding rankings presented in table 4-11.

One surprising fact immediately apparent is that even though Brazil had

Table 4-11. Index of real wages in the overall industrial sample for LAFTA countries in November 1966, adjusted by size of firm
(LAFTA average = 100)

Country	Index	Rank
Argentina	80	(7)
Bolivia	101	(3)
Brazil	54	(11)
Chile	75	(9)
Colombia	99	(5)
Ecuador	58	(10)
Mexico	159	(1)
Paraguay	79	(8)
Peru	91	(6)
Uruguay	100	(4)
Venezuela	120	(2)
Coefficient of Variation = 0.3039		

extreme values in one industry, this did not seem to affect the overall index in an important fashion; thus, Brazil ranks last. This is due to the relatively lesser importance of the metallurgical industry in LAFTA as a whole,[21] and to the decrease in Brazilian wage relatives in the other industries, as size of firm is adjusted for.

If the rankings in table 4-11 are composed with the standings, not including the size of firm adjustment (see table 4-10), a substantial alteration is noted. The wage differentials are even more drastically changed. Just to note the most salient cases, Venezuela is only about 20% above the LAFTA average after size of firm is normalized, while the net effect of the size of firm adjustment in the case of Brazil is to drop its wages to just above half the LAFTA average.

The disparity in real wages between the low extreme (Brazil and Ecuador) and the high (Mexico) increases after the size of the firm has been accounted for. On the other hand, wage differences among the other countries decrease significantly. The overall dispersion, as noted by the coefficient of variation, diminishes after the size of firm adjustment.

When wages are not adjusted they represent a very crude measure of the take-home pay of workers in various countries. As job content variables are included, the comparison comes closer to the concept of wages adjusted by productivity factors. After considering the several qualitative elements, it has been seen that for those countries where high wages were tied to high intrinsic productivity of labor in some industries, the adjustments have diminished their relative wage levels vis-à-vis the rest of LAFTA. The opposite has occurred in those countries where high levels were not tied to high values of the qualitative variables.[22]

Although the factors considered here are mainly related to intrinsic labor productivity, at least the size of the firm is connected to overall labor productivity. Moreover, when the job content of occupations is demanding, as expressed in terms of qualitative variables, and the size of the firm is large, this is probably tied to high capital-labor ratios, advanced technology, and so forth. This is due to the fact that to work with more capital and to apply more refined techniques, better labor is usually required. Thus, the effects of some of these other variables are implicitly considered when the factors introduced in the proceding analysis are accounted for. Yet, it is expected

21. Even if each country's weights had been used, the results would have been the same, because in Brazil this industry is smaller than in the other two.

22. The same reasoning holds for the relationships between low wages and intrinsic productivity. For example, the wages of low wage countries with low values in their qualitative requirements would be raised after normalization.

that some of the unexplained wage variation could be further reduced if those other factors affecting overall labor productivity were explicitly considered.[23] In the next chapter some of these ideas will be explored further and their consequences for trade and efficient allocation within LAFTA discussed.

23. The potentially exporting and supposedly most efficient firms within each country were selected in the sample. Thus, the intercountry effects of these other factors have been neutralized to an important degree in this study.

Chapter 5. Intercountry labor cost differentials

This chapter presents a comparative examination of labor costs in LAFTA countries. Labor cost is defined as straight wages, year-end bonuses, profit-sharing arrangements, family allowances, and employer's social security contributions. Also included is an adjustment for the difference in vacation and holiday pay in the various countries.

Labor costs are compared in money terms; they are converted into a common currency by the use of the official rather than the purchasing power parity exchange rates. This is because the labor cost comparisons are used for an examination of cost advantage and potential trade flows within the region. For such purposes the rates that determine intercountry trade and exchange are the relevant ones. It is usually on the basis of the officially set rates of foreign exchange that traders decide what to export and import.[1]

The methodology and procedures used in this chapter are the same as those in the previous one. Stepwise regression equations were run with logs of wages as the dependent variable, and the qualitative job requirements, intercept country dummies, and slope country dummies as the independent variables. A particular step was chosen on the basis of the previously discussed criteria, and from the corresponding regression equation, wages corresponding to the quartile combinations of qualitative variables were estimated. From these, wage relative indices and rankings were constructed. The results differ from the previous ones basically in terms of the wage concept used, and therefore the regression equations and the quartile levels of the independent variables will not be reproduced here.

The textile industry

In table 5-1 the labor costs by quartile are presented for the textile industry. These quartile wages are then averaged in geometric fashion, by applying the weights used previously. The results are presented in table 5-2.

---

1. If optimal allocation for LAFTA as a whole were the objective of the study, equilibrium or shadow rates of exchange would be preferable. However, these are difficult to ascertain in any case.

Table 5-1. Estimated money labor costs per hour in the textile industry for each LAFTA country, November 1966[a]

Country	1st Quartile			2nd Quartile			3rd Quartile		
	Absolute ($)	Relative (%)	Rank	Absolute ($)	Relative (%)	Rank	Absolute ($)	Relative (%)	Rank
Argentina	0.69	133	(2)	0.94	125	(3)	1.29	117	(4)
Bolivia	0.31	60	(10)	0.39	52	(10)	0.47	43	(11)
Brazil	0.44	85	(8)	0.68	91	(8)	1.05	95	(6)
Chile	0.67	129	(3)	1.01	135	(1)	1.54	140	(1)
Colombia	0.41	79	(9)	0.64	85	(9)	0.97	88	(8)
Ecuador	0.20	38	(11)	0.35	47	(11)	0.59	54	(10)
Mexico	0.71	137	(1)	0.83	111	(5)	0.97	88	(8)
Paraguay	0.49	94	(7)	0.75	100	(7)	1.15	105	(5)
Peru	0.59	113	(5)	0.92	123	(4)	1.50	136	(3)
Uruguay	0.57	110	(6)	0.78	104	(6)	1.05	95	(6)
Venezuela	0.65	125	(4)	1.00	133	(2)	1.51	137	(2)
LAFTA average	0.52	100		0.75	100		1.10	100	
Coefficient of variation	0.3050			0.2853			0.3074		

Kendall coefficient of concordance = 0.8682 at the 0.01 level of significance.

[a] Converted into U.S. dollars by using official exchange rates for November 1966, as published in the International Monetary Fund, *International Financial Statistics* (Washington, D.C., I.M.F., 1967). The figures correspond to money labor costs and are adjusted to a common job content across countries.

Table 5-2. Index of money labor costs in the textile
industry for LAFTA countries, November 1966
(LAFTA average = 100)

Country	Index	Rank
Argentina	125	(3)
Bolivia	51	(10)
Brazil	91	(8)
Chile	135	(1)
Colombia	84	(9)
Ecuador	47	(11)
Mexico	109	(5)
Paraguay	100	(7)
Peru	124	(4)
Uruguay	103	(6)
Venezuela	132	(2)
Coefficient of Variation = 0.2871		

Table 5-1 shows that the rankings and differentials vary greatly by quartile, evincing the importance of the slope dummies and the necessity of a comparison at different levels of education, experience, and responsibility to obtain a reliable estimate of intercountry wage differentials.[2]

Table 5-2, where the overall industry results are shown, makes clear that the results in terms of labor costs are substantially different from those based on wages or take-home pay. Only part of this can be explained in terms of the difference in the exchange rate used for conversion purposes.[3] It can be seen that in terms of labor costs it is not just Peru and Venezuela but also Chile and Argentina that have the highest rankings (there is very little difference among these four countries) in table 5-2.

Other changes affect Mexico and Uruguay, with the position of the former falling and that of the latter rising relative to the take-home pay results. Brazil improves its ranking, with the opposite happening to Colombia, while the positions of Bolivia and Ecuador remain unchanged. Also, the dispersion of money labor costs within LAFTA is less than that of wages or

2. For an examination of the interquartile spread for each industry, and a comparison of the results at the different quartile levels, see chapter 4. The conclusions in terms of labor costs do not differ significantly from those presented there.

3. This was established by comparing labor costs and wages in money terms, which use the official rates of exchange for conversion purposes. For the money wages results see the appendix to this chapter.

Table 5-3. Estimated money labor costs per hour in the pharmaceutical industry for each LAFTA country, November 1966[a]

Country	1st Quartile			2nd Quartile			3rd Quartile		
	Absolute ($)	Relative (%)	Rank	Absolute ($)	Relative (%)	Rank	Absolute ($)	Relative (%)	Rank
Argentina	0.77	138	(2)	0.87	114	(2)	0.97	92	(6)
Bolivia	0.50	89	(5)	0.63	83	(6)	0.79	75	(7)
Brazil	0.54	96	(4)	0.79	104	(4)	1.18	101	(4)
Chile	0.67	120	(3)	0.84	111	(3)	1.06	100	(5)
Colombia	0.49	88	(6)	0.74	97	(5)	1.12	106	(2)
Ecuador	0.42	75	(8)	0.51	67	(9)	0.62	58	(9)
Mexico	-	-	-	-	-	-	-	-	-
Paraguay	0.39	70	(9)	0.48	63	(10)	0.59	56	(10)
Peru	0.29	52	(10)	0.58	76	(7)	1.10	104	(3)
Uruguay	0.46	82	(7)	0.58	76	(7)	0.74	70	(8)
Venezuela	1.09	195	(1)	1.61	212	(1)	2.39	225	(1)
LAFTA average	0.56	100		0.76	100		1.06	100	
Coefficient of variation	0.3887			0.4070			0.4625		

Kendall coefficient of concordance = 0.8272 at the 0.01 level of significance.

[a] For notes see table 5-1. Because of reasons cited before, Mexico could not be included in the comparisons in this industry.

Table 5-4. Index of money labor costs in the
pharmaceutical industry for LAFTA countries,
November 1966
(LAFTA average = 100)

Country	Index	Rank
Argentina	107	(2)
Bolivia	80	(7)
Brazil	102	(4)
Chile	107	(2)
Colombia	99	(5)
Ecuador	64	(9)
Mexico	-	-
Paraguay	61	(10)
Peru	83	(6)
Uruguay	74	(8)
Venezuela	215	(1)
Coefficient of Variation = 0.4217		

take-home pay when the latter are expressed in money terms (the coefficients of variation are 0.29 and 0.32, respectively), with most countries being relatively close together except for Bolivia and Ecuador.[4]

The pharmaceutical industry

The same type of basic data are presented for the pharmaceutical industry in tables 5-3 and 5-4. In this industry, the rankings and differentials are again altered, if contrasted with the net wage comparisons of chapter 4. Labor costs in the pharmaceutical industry of Venezuela are clearly the highest in LAFTA, being more than twice the average for all LAFTA countries. On the other hand, Ecuador and Paraguay have the lowest labor costs in the area. The rankings and relatives of these countries at both extremes of the intercountry comparison coincide with those shown in terms of take-home pay, after the difference in conversion factors is taken into account. However, many changes can be noted for the rest of the countries, which are relatively close to each other. In particular, Argentina, Brazil, Chile, and Uruguay have substantially improved their relative standing vis-à-vis Colombia and Peru. Hence, as in the textile industry, the only extreme deviants in the scale are the very high and low countries. Finally, the dispersion in the labor cost indices for the industry is also smaller than that

4. See appendix to this chapter for the industry wage (take-home pay) indices expressed in money terms.

Table 5-5. Estimated money labor costs per hour in the metallurgical industry for each LAFTA country, November 1966[a]

Country	1st Quartile			2nd Quartile			3rd Quartile		
	Absolute ($)	Relative (%)	Rank	Absolute ($)	Relative (%)	Rank	Absolute ($)	Relative (%)	Rank
Argentina	0.89	165	(2)	1.21	145	(3)	1.83	150	(3)
Bolivia	-	-	-	-	-	-	-	-	-
Brazil	0.62	115	(4)	0.75	91	(5)	1.01	83	(6)
Chile	0.42	78	(6)	1.48	180	(1)	1.85	152	(2)
Colombia	0.35	65	(7)	0.57	70	(7)	1.01	83	(6)
Ecuador	0.12	22	(10)	0.23	28	(10)	0.60	49	(9)
Mexico	1.27	235	(1)	1.36	166	(2)	1.46	120	(4)
Paraguay	0.23	43	(9)	0.33	40	(9)	0.52	43	(10)
Peru	0.24	44	(8)	0.46	56	(8)	1.08	89	(5)
Uruguay	0.44	81	(5)	0.60	73	(6)	0.89	73	(8)
Venezuela	0.83	154	(3)	1.19	145	(4)	1.95	160	(1)
LAFTA average	0.54	100		0.82	100		1.22	100	
Coefficient of variation	0.6319			0.5257			0.4057		

Kendall coefficient of concordance = 0.8407 at the 0.01 level of significance.

[a]For notes see table 5-1. Because of the reasons cited earlier, Bolivia was not included in the comparisons of this industry.

Table 5-6. Index of money labor costs in the
metallurgical industry for LAFTA countries,
November 1966
(LAFTA average = 100)

Country	Index	Rank
Argentina	151	(3)
Bolivia	-	-
Brazil	91	(5)
Chile	153	(2)
Colombia	73	(7)
Ecuador	33	(10)
Mexico	156	(1)
Paraguay	41	(9)
Peru	63	(8)
Uruguay	74	(6)
Venezuela	151	(3)
Coefficient of Variation = 0.4751		

of take-home pay, expressed in money terms (coefficients of variation are
0.4217 and 0.4941 respectively).[5]

The metallurgical industry

As with the first two industries, there are significant changes in the rankings and in the wage relatives across quartiles for the metallurgical industry. Actually such variations seem to be most acute in this industry.[6]

The overall index for the metallurgical industry shows four countries
with labor costs 50% above those of the LAFTA average. Except for one,
these are the same high labor cost countries encountered in the textile comparison (Venezuela, Argentina, and Chile), with Mexico replacing Peru at
the high end of the scale in this case. As in the pharmaceutical industry,
Ecuador and Paraguay are the countries with lowest labor costs. In comparison with the other two industries, much wider labor cost disparities can
be noted in the metallurgical industry (see the coefficient of variation in
table 5-6).

5. See the appendix to this chapter for the take-home pay in money terms presented in
index form.
6. If the average LAFTA money labor costs are compared on an industry by industry basis, a
remarkable coincidence emerges. The first and second quartile labor costs are almost the same
in the three industries. Third quartile wages are not so close, basically because of the metallurgical industry. The latter appears to have higher labor costs overall, especially if the less
demanding quartile sets of qualitative requirements are considered.

Contrasting the results in terms of wages or take-home pay with the corresponding ones presented in this chapter, the changes in rankings and differentials can be ascertained. Labor costs for Mexico and Venezuela do not depart as far from the LAFTA average as is the case for take-home pay. Peru and Colombia also experience some relative decline when labor costs are considered, while those of Chile increase considerably. No variation takes place in the lower end of the scale, where Ecuador and Paraguay still hold their wage differentials.

Dispersion in the wage scales appears to be smaller in terms of labor costs (see coefficient of variation in table 5-6 vis-à-vis coefficient of variation in the appendix to this chapter). This was also the case in the textile and pharmaceutical industries. Given that fringe benefits are partial substitutes for straight wages, it would be expected that labor cost differentials would be narrower than wage or take-home pay differentials, as experienced in the three industries examined.

The overall industrial sample

By combining the labor costs levels of each country in the various industries and weighting them in terms of value added by the relative importance of each industry for LAFTA as a whole, a combined index of labor costs can be constructed. Such a formulation summarizes the comparisons presented above on an industry by industry basis and constitutes an overall measure of the labor cost advantages and disadvantages of the countries in question for the three industries considered. The results are presented in table 5-7.

Obviously Venezuela is an extreme on the high side and Ecuador and Bolivia are extremes on the low side. Comparing these results with the overall wage comparisons presented in the previous chapter, it is apparent that the position of Bolivia and Ecuador have not changed much, while Venezuela's differential with respect to the other LAFTA countries has been compressed somewhat.

The positions of the Southern Cone Industries of Chile, Argentina, Brazil, and Uruguay rise when labor costs are compared. Chile raises its relative position the most (about 30% overall) if labor costs are compared rather than money wages. Argentina, Brazil, and Uruguay follow in that order, with the latter raising its position about 15%. On the other hand, Mexico, Peru, and Colombia suffer a fall in their relative positions when labor cost comparisons are introduced. Such changes in the LAFTA relatives bring about alterations in the rankings of these countries.

It appears that when further fringe benefits are included and deductions for social security contributions are eliminated, transforming take-home pay into labor costs, the experience of the Southern Cone countries in

Table 5-7. Index of money labor costs in the overall
industrial sample for LAFTA countries, November 1966
(LAFTA average = 100)

Country	Index	Rank
Argentina	121	(3)
Bolivia	61	(10)
Brazil	95	(6)
Chile	126	(2)
Colombia	88	(7)
Ecuador	51	(11)
Mexico	117	(4)
Paraguay	75	(9)
Peru	99	(5)
Uruguay	88	(7)
Venezuela	160	(1)
Coefficient of Variation	= 0.3042	

LAFTA differs considerably from those of the northern countries. Hence, what explains the substantial modification in the rankings and relative wage differentials is that the countries in the former group appear to have a more comprehensive system of social and fringe benefits, mostly implanted by law. The northern countries (Venezuela, Mexico, Colombia, and Peru) appear to stress higher straight wages, probably resulting from less governmental intervention and more direct union influence. Ecuador, Bolivia, and Paraguay, the poorest countries in LAFTA, appear to be in an intermediate position in terms of the importance of social benefits in total wage payments.

The latter countries seem to have had considerable labor cost advantages[7] in the LAFTA modern manufacturing sector at the end of 1966, if the three industries considered are a good indication.[8] Moreover, the dispersion in the labor cost indices suggests that there might have been profitable opportunities for Ecuador, Bolivia, and Paraguay to export products of

7. Meaning lower labor costs for undertaking representative tasks with workers of uniform quality.

8. This is assuming that labor costs in the rest of the modern manufacturing sector do not diverge radically from those examined in the survey. It has been pointed out before that the levels do not differ greatly between the three industries considered and the nine industries covered in the national chapters (see chapters 7 and 8 and the appendix at the end of the book). Given that the sample survey is representative, especially of the modern manufacting sector, the findings for these three industries can be generalized to cover the latter.

these industries to other countries in the area. It should be stressed however, that labor cost advantages are not tantamount to trade advantages. The former only indicate potential trade advantages. This results from the fact that labor costs are just one of the determinants—albeit a major one—of trade advantages. Other determinants may more than compensate for relatively low or high labor costs in particular countries. What all this means is that the labor costs here presented may diverge from labor costs per unit output, and even more from total costs per unit. This must be borne in mind in the conjectural analysis that follows.

Ecuador, Bolivia, and Paraguay had levels of labor costs ranging from 50% to 25% below the LAFTA average. There was even a significant spread among the labor costs of these three countries, with Ecuador having the lowest costs and Paraguay the highest of the three. Uruguay, Colombia, Brazil, and Peru follow, although there is not a significant difference among the labor costs of these four countries. Given their higher levels of development and of technological sophistication, as well as their probably lower capital costs, these four countries would appear to have been strong competitors with Ecuador, Bolivia, and Paraguay as potential exporters of manufactured products to the rest of LAFTA at the end of 1966.

In contrast, it would appear that the positions of Argentina, Mexico, and Chile, having labor costs which were approximately two times those of the countries with the lowest levels of development, were not very promising within the context of LAFTA. However, the fact that Argentina and Mexico have been able to export manufactured products to LAFTA suggests that, even after adjustment for job content, the other determinants of trade advantages (like capital costs, overall productivity, supply availability, and demand conditions) have over-compensated for lower labor costs in certain cases.

All considered, Brazil and, to a certain extent, Colombia seem to have had slight advantages as potential exporters within LAFTA at the end of 1966; both had relatively low labor costs. While Brazil has already shown its capacity to export manufactures, Colombia is just beginning to do so. However, another factor that has to be considered is that, as has been found previously in an ECIEL-Brookings study of industrial location, potential trade advantages seem to vary greatly across industries.[9] Thus even Venezuela, the highest labor cost country within LAFTA, may have a potential advantage in certain lines, like petrochemicals.

---

9. See the ECIEL study prepared by Martin Carnoy, *Industrialization in a Latin American Common Market* (Washington, D.C.: Brookings Institution, 1972).

Labor costs adjusted by the effects of size of firm

In the previous chapter it was seen that firm size had a profound influence on wage differentials and standings. It would be interesting to briefly consider how labor cost comparisons would be affected by the introduction of this variable. The same *caveat* mentioned in the last section of the previous chapter would hold; briefly restated, the results are not as reliable as those just adjusting for education, experience, and responsibility. They are only presented to illustrate the effect of size of firm, and even then only because they might be useful to some researchers. They should be interpreted with care.

The purpose here is not to analyze the effect of size of firm on the results for its own sake, as this was done in chapter 4. It is rather to consider how such alterations affect the conclusions derived previously with respect to labor cost advantages and trade within LAFTA.

As before, the three industrial indices can be combined into an overall index of labor costs after size of firm adjustments. From table 5-8 it can be seen that Venezuela has the highest place in the scale, followed at considerable distance by Mexico and Argentina. Ecuador and then Paraguay appear to have the lowest labor costs in LAFTA, with Colombia not far behind. The rest of the countries appear to have very similar labor costs.

Table 5-8. Index of money labor costs in the overall
industrial sample for LAFTA countries, November 1966,
adjusted for size of firm
(LAFTA average = 100)

Country	Index	Rank
Argentina	107	(3)
Bolivia	99	(4)
Brazil	84	(7)
Chile	90	(5)
Colombia	74	(9)
Ecuador	50	(11)
Mexico	118	(2)
Paraguay	70	(10)
Peru	87	(6)
Uruguay	81	(8)
Venezuela	140	(1)
Coefficient of Variation = 0.2574		

After taking into consideration the effects of firm size, it would appear that Ecuador may have had the best potential to exploit its lower labor costs and translate them into export opportunities for manufactured products within LAFTA.[10] It is reassuring that the poor and small countries, which would need solid trade concessions if a working LAFTA is to develop, apparently were mostly the countries with labor cost advantages in these industries. Of course, other cost disadvantages or overall productivity differentials may overwhelm their low labor costs. However, technological and mechanization levels in the modern manufacturing sector may not be that different throughout Latin America. This may contribute to make the productivity of labor resulting from the use of capital and technology very similar. As a result the cost of other factors of production may not differ greatly among these countries. This is especially the case when labor costs have been adjusted by job content and size of firm, which can be interpreted as a way of partially homogenizing the effects of capital and technology on the comparisons.[11] Yet, there are other factors on the supply side (like deficient marketing know-how) which may neutralize the labor costs advantages noted.

Even though their labor costs are somewhat higher, it would appear that Colombia and Brazil also had favorable export prospects at the end of 1966, given their higher levels of industrialization and development, their much larger markets, which would provide for a more fruitful exploitation of economies of scale, and their better marketing know-how. On the other hand, Mexico, and especially Venezuela, did not appear to have labor cost levels that would suggest export possibilities within the LAFTA area at the time.

However, all of these conclusions must be qualified. As pointed out before, labor costs seem to differ importantly from industry to industry. In fact, this reaches the point of affecting the country rankings of the three industries considered in terms of labor costs levels. If this is the case, even a high labor cost country like Venezuela, and more possibly Mexico, may have had lower wage relatives in certain industrial lines whose products they could potentially export to the rest of LAFTA.

In short, the apparent labor cost advantages, and thus the potential trade advantages, that the smaller and less developed countries in LAFTA appeared to have at the end of 1966, were significantly reduced by the size of

10. The country labor cost levels in the other industries included in the survey (see table 3-1) support this, as they are comparable to those in the textile, pharmaceutical, and metallurgical industries.

11. Larger firms and more demanding job contents are usually related to a greater use of capital and of modern techniques.

firm adjustment, except in the case of Ecuador. On the other hand, the size of the firm adjustment generally lowered the wage relatives of the larger and more developed LAFTA countries, thus improving the potentially favorable positions of Colombia and Brazil and reducing the apparent disadvantages of the high labor cost countries, like Venezuela. In the final chapter, where the policy implications of the study are drawn out, this theme is touched upon again, based on extrapolations of these data to more recent dates.

Appendix 5-1. Money-wage comparisons

Table 5-9. Index of money wages in the textile industry
for LAFTA countries, November 1966
(LAFTA average = 100)

Country	Index	Rank
Argentina	103	(5)
Bolivia	46	(11)
Brazil	78	(9)
Chile	113	(4)
Colombia	94	(7)
Ecuador	48	(10)
Mexico	125	(3)
Paraguay	102	(6)
Peru	146	(2)
Uruguay	91	(8)
Venezuela	147	(1)
Coefficient of Variation = 0.3232		

Table 5-10. Index of money wages in the pharmaceutical
industry for LAFTA countries,
November 1966
(LAFTA average = 100)

Country	Index	Rank
Argentina	95	(4)
Bolivia	83	(7)
Brazil	90	(5)
Chile	87	(6)
Colombia	110	(2)
Ecuador	65	(8)
Mexico	-	-
Paraguay	62	(10)
Peru	96	(3)
Uruguay	64	(9)
Venezuela	239	(1)
Coefficient of Variation = 0.4941		

Table 5-11. Index of money wages in the metallurgical
industry for LAFTA countries, November 1966
(LAFTA average = 100)

Country	Index	Rank
Argentina	143	(3)
Bolivia	-	-
Brazil	81	(5)
Chile	74	(7)
Colombia	86	(4)
Ecuador	36	(10)
Mexico	195	(1)
Paraguay	45	(9)
Peru	78	(6)
Uruguay	70	(8)
Venezuela	175	(2)
Coefficient of Variation = 0.5207		

Table 5-12. Index of money wages in the overall
industrial sample for LAFTA countries, November 1966
(LAFTA average = 100)

Country	Index	Rank
Argentina	104	(4)
Bolivia	58	(10)
Brazil	83	(7)
Chile	98	(6)
Colombia	99	(5)
Ecuador	52	(11)
Mexico	138	(2)
Paraguay	78	(8)
Peru	117	(3)
Uruguay	78	(8)
Venezuela	179	(1)
Coefficient of Variation = 0.3528		

Chapter 6. Intercountry pay differentials for the same position

This chapter examines the extent to which pay differentials exist among countries for the same position after the impact of qualitative requirements has been accounted for. The positions covered in this chapter were only those for which sufficient observations were obtained in the countries covered. As will be recalled, two types of positions were surveyed in the study: "key" positions, which were included and defined beforehand, and other positions, whose inclusion and definition were determined at the time of the survey and which were not uniformly covered across countries and industries. Only the key positions are covered in this chapter, subclassified into two groups: clerical positions and production positions. One of the latter, engineering trainee, had to be omitted because such data did not exist in a number of the sampled firms. For each of the eleven remaining positions, an index measuring intercountry differentials will be shown and commented upon in the following pages, with the LAFTA average as the base.

Clerical positions

Five such positions were covered—file clerk, typist, invoice clerk, accounting clerk, and cashier—and are defined in appendix 2 of chapter 3. Table 6-1 presents the index corresponding to file clerk. The concept used in the comparisons is that of net wages or take-home pay expressed in real terms (utilizing purchasing power parity rates for conversion into a common currency). The same four variables as before were used for normalization purposes: education, experience, responsibility, and the size of firm.

As table 6-1 makes evident, Mexico, Peru, and Venezuela are the countries in which file clerks receive the highest wages in real terms, but with Mexico 50% above the other two. In contrast, real wages for file clerks are the lowest in Brazil. In the rest of the countries the real wage levels of file clerks are not that far apart.

In table 6-2 comparable results are presented for typists. Again Mexico is highest, followed at a distance by Venezuela and Chile. As in the pre-

Table 6-1. Index of real wages for file clerks in the
overall industrial sample, November 1966
(LAFTA average = 100)

Country	Index	Rank
Argentina[a]	71	(7)
Bolivia[a]	63	(10)
Brazil	36	(11)
Chile	99	(4)
Colombia	90	(5)
Ecuador[a]	70	(9)
Mexico	224	(1)
Paraguay	71	(7)
Peru	149	(2)
Uruguay	85	(6)
Venezuela	149	(2)
Coefficient of Variation = 0.51		

[a]These countries did not report a sufficient number of observations for this position to be included in the various industry regressions. Thus, the index numbers presented here partly result from imputations.

vious case, there is a wide divergence among the wage levels of the three top countries, with Mexican wages being almost double those of Chile and 50% over those of Venezuela. Brazil is again lowest in real terms. Contrastingly, Peru, which pays file clerks very well, seems to have a low pay scale for typists, ranking only slightly ahead of Brazil. Again, the spread among the rest of the countries in the scale is relatively small.

For invoice clerk, once again Mexico, Venezuela, and Peru pay the highest real wages (table 6-3). Brazil once more has the lowest remuneration in this position, with Bolivia only somewhat higher. Figures for the six countries occupying the middle positions are close, although the pattern is somewhat different this time. The dispersion patterns among the high, middle, and low groups of countries range considerably less than those for file clerks and typists, having the lowest variation of the clerical positions.

Some of the same countries appear again with very high real wages for accounting clerks (see table 6-4). Mexico and Venezuela still have the highest real wage levels, followed by Chile. At the other end of the scale Bolivia and Peru have very low index values of 27 and 44 respectively. The disparities here are even greater than in previously examined positions. Wage levels in the countries ranking at the top are about five times

Table 6-2. Index of real wages for typists in the overall
industrial sample, November 1966
(LAFTA average = 100)

Country	Index	Rank
Argentina[a]	77	(8)
Bolivia	71	(9)
Brazil	47	(11)
Chile	118	(3)
Colombia	99	(4)
Ecuador	81	(6)
Mexico	229	(1)
Paraguay	79	(7)
Peru	52	(10)
Uruguay	91	(5)
Venezuela	158	(2)
Coefficient of Variation = 0.50		

[a]This country did not contain a sufficient number of observations
for this position to be included in the various industry regressions.
Thus, the index numbers presented here partly result from imputations.

Table 6-3. Index of real wages for invoice clerks in the
overall industrial sample, November 1966
(LAFTA average = 100)

Country	Index	Rank
Argentina[a]	74	(9)
Bolivia	64	(10)
Brazil	55	(11)
Chile	100	(4)
Colombia	95	(5)
Ecuador	78	(8)
Mexico	187	(1)
Paraguay	94	(6)
Peru	135	(2)
Uruguay[a]	89	(7)
Venezuela	131	(3)
Coefficient of Variation = 0.36		

[a]These countries did not contain a sufficient number of observations for this position, and thus could not be included in the various
country regressions. As a result, the index number presented here
partly results from imputations.

Table 6-4. Index of real wages for accounting clerks in
the overall industrial sample, November 1966
(LAFTA average = 100)

Country	Index	Rank
Argentina	81	(5)
Bolivia	27	(11)
Brazil	78	(7)
Chile	164	(3)
Colombia	58	(9)
Ecuador	60	(8)
Mexico	213	(1)
Paraguay	80	(6)
Peru	44	(10)
Uruguay	96	(4)
Venezuela	202	(2)
Coefficient of Variation = 0.60		

Table 6-5. Index of real wages for cashiers in the overall
industrial sample, November 1966
(LAFTA average = 100)

Country	Index	Rank
Argentina	68	(9)
Bolivia	53	(10)
Brazil	77	(8)
Chile	161	(2)
Colombia	97	(5)
Ecuador	51	(11)
Mexico	171	(1)
Paraguay	88	(6)
Peru	104	(4)
Uruguay	82	(7)
Venezuela	150	(3)
Coefficient of Variation = 0.40		

greater than in those ranking at the bottom, with a less apparent concentration of real wage levels in between.

The last clerical position to be covered is that of cashier (see table 6-5). In contrast with the pattern of dispersion found for accounting clerks, the real wages in this occupation appear to be relatively concentrated. The range of dispersion is one of the smallest among the clerical positions.

Table 6-6. Index of real wages for janitors in the overall
industrial sample, November 1966
(LAFTA average = 100)

Country	Index	Rank
Argentina	165	(3)
Bolivia	31	(10)
Brazil	22	(11)
Chile	63	(7)
Colombia	92	(5)
Ecuador	41	(9)
Mexico	202	(1)
Paraguay	76	(6)
Peru	63	(7)
Uruguay	200	(2)
Venezuela	135	(4)
Coefficient of Variation = 0.63		

Mexico, Chile, and Venezuela have the highest real wages, while Ecuador
and Bolivia have the lowest. The wages for the rest of the countries are not
as close to each other as in previous positions, but present a more concentrated pattern than in the case of accounting clerks.

In summary, the intercountry comparisons for clerical employees seem
to indicate that Mexico and Venezuela have consistently the highest wage
levels for this type of position, with Chile and Peru following. The countries with lowest real wages for these positions are generally Brazil and
Bolivia.[1] Although changing, the rankings of most positions are quite consistent for the countries mentioned, with the exception of Peru. For that
country, wages oscillated between very high and very low rankings, which
suggests significantly higher interoccupational variation.

Production positions

Six positions are covered here: janitor, machinist, lathe operator, maintenance electrician, truck driver, and foreman. Wage differential data for the
first of these positions, janitor, are shown in table 6-6. For this position,
the country rankings differ somewhat from those characterizing the clerical
workers discussed in the previous section. The highest real take-home pay

1. Keep in mind that there are reasons to suspect that the ECLA extrapolations of the purchasing power parity exchange rates bias downwards the level of real wages in Brazil. The
opposite occurs in the case of Chile.

for janitors is again found in Mexico, which also pays the highest wages in clerical positions, but now Uruguay as well as Argentina are in the top spots.

Bolivia and Brazil are again at the lower end of the scale, with unusually low real-wage levels. No other position shows up in such extreme fashion for the low ranking countries. The spread is also wider among the middle countries for this position when compared to previous ones.

The comparison of real-wage levels for operators of industrial machines (machinists) shows Mexico on top, followed by Uruguay, and then at a considerable distance, Venezuela (table 6-7). There is a substantial difference between Mexico and the other two countries. Bolivia, Brazil, and Ecuador are at the lower end of the scale, and the rest of the countries are relatively close together.

For lathe operators (table 6-8), Uruguayan and Mexican levels are about 60% above those of LAFTA, while the two countries that follow, Venezuela and Peru, are relatively close to the LAFTA average. Bolivia and Ecuador pay the lowest real wages to lathe operators after normalization. The index range for this position is narrow, with the ratio of the highest to the lowest country wages being about four, and the coefficient of variation 0.40.

Table 6-7. Index of real wages for machinists in the overall industrial sample, November 1966
(LAFTA average = 100)

Country	Index	Rank
Argentina	100	(4)
Bolivia[a]	38	(10)
Brazil	38	(10)
Chile	68	(8)
Colombia	86	(6)
Ecuador	58	(9)
Mexico	229	(1)
Paraguay	76	(7)
Peru	89	(5)
Uruguay[a]	200	(2)
Venezuela	113	(3)
Coefficient of Variation = 0.59		

[a]The number of observations for machinists in these countries was too few to be included in the various country regressions. Thus, the index numbers for these countries are partly the result of imputations.

Table 6-8. Index of real wages for lathe operators in the
overall industrial sample, November 1966
(LAFTA average = 100)

Country	Index	Rank
Argentina[a]	79	(7)
Bolivia	40	(11)
Brazil	76	(9)
Chile	79	(7)
Colombia	81	(6)
Ecuador	58	(10)
Mexico	163	(2)
Paraguay	93	(5)
Peru[a]	130	(4)
Uruguay[a]	164	(1)
Venezuela	136	(3)
Coefficient of Variation = 0.40		

[a]The number of observations for lathe operators in these countries was too few to be included in the various country regressions. Thus, the index number for these countries are partly the result of imputations.

Thus, the real wage variation among lathe operators is much smaller than that for machinists.

The comparison of real wages for maintenance electricians (table 6-9) shows Mexico, Uruguay, and Venezuela topping the other countries. As a group, these three countries are well above the rest of LAFTA, and hence this position registers one of the highest intercountry wage differentials in any position examined so far. Bolivia and Ecuador have the lowest wages for electricians.

For truck drivers, Mexico, Ecuador, and Uruguay appear to have the highest real wages in LAFTA (table 6-10). In this occupation the intercountry wages differentials at the high side of the scale are relatively narrow. At the low end of the scale, Bolivia and Paraguay occupy the two bottom places, with deviations similar to those found for other production jobs.

The last production job, that of foreman, presents some surprising results (table 6-11). For one, Uruguay is the country topping the list, followed by Venezuela, with Mexico third. On the other hand, the pay of foremen in Bolivia appears to be remarkably low. Ecuador and Brazil follow this country in the standings. Although the dispersion in this occupation is not the widest among those examined here, i.e., coefficient of variation of

0.53, the ratio of highest to lowest wages is far above any of the others. The average of the three highest countries is over four times the average level of the three countries at the bottom of the standings.

Considering the various real-wage indices for production workers it would appear that Mexico pays the highest wages overall. Venezuela is not only below Mexico but also Uruguay in the overall standings. Looking at the rankings of the various positions from the bottom up, Bolivia is clearly the country with lower real pay for production workers. Brazil, Ecuador, and Paraguay follow closely bunched together, at the next higher step in the scale. The standings were mostly consistent for the countries at the high and low ends of the rankings with few major changes occurring from one position to the other.

There was more variation in the wage indices of the six production jobs just examined than in the indices for clerical positions. For some occupations, the dispersion was very high (i.e., electricians, janitors, and foremen) while for others it was the opposite (i.e., truck drivers and lathe operators). The pattern of high, middle, and low countries was less easily recognized than in the clerical positions and the relationships emerging

Table 6-9. Index of real wages for maintenance
electricians in the overall industrial sample,
November 1966
(LAFTA average = 100)

Country	Index	Rank
Argentina[a]	88	(5)
Bolivia	27	(11)
Brazil	49	(9)
Chile[a]	76	(6)
Colombia	68	(7)
Ecuador	41	(10)
Mexico	215	(1)
Paraguay	54	(8)
Peru	126	(4)
Uruguay[a]	184	(2)
Venezuela	176	(3)
Coefficient of Variation = 0.62		

[a]The number of observations for electricians in these countries was too few to be included in the various country regressions. Thus, the index number for these countries are partly the result of imputations.

Table 6-10. Index of real wages for truck drivers in the
overall industrial sample, November 1966
(LAFTA average = 100)

Country	Index	Rank
Argentina	72	(8)
Bolivia	38	(11)
Brazil	105	(5)
Chile[a]	83	(7)
Colombia	71	(9)
Ecuador	154	(2)
Mexico	155	(1)
Paraguay[a]	50	(10)
Peru	97	(6)
Uruguay	150	(3)
Venezuela	128	(4)
Coefficient of Variation = 0.40		

[a]The number of observations for truckers in these countries was
too few to be included in the various country regressions. Thus, the
index number for these countries are partly the result of imputations.

Table 6-11. Index of real wages for foremen in the overall
industrial sample, November 1966
(LAFTA average = 100)

Country	Index	Rank
Argentina[a]	83	(7)
Bolivia	18	(11)
Brazil[a]	55	(9)
Chile	108	(5)
Colombia	88	(6)
Ecuador[a]	47	(10)
Mexico	152	(3)
Paraguay	65	(8)
Peru[a]	112	(4)
Uruguay	198	(1)
Venezuela	169	(2)
Coefficient of Variation = 0.53		

[a]The number of observations for foremen in these countries was
quite restricted and as a result it could not be included in the various
country regressions performed. Thus, the index number for these
countries are partly the result of imputations.

among groups of countries were less uniform. However, Kendall's coefficient of concordance is 0.78 among production positions, 0.76 for clerical positions, and 0.69 for all positions combined; all of these coefficients are statistically significant at the 0.01 level.

Overall results

Data on the relative importance of each of these jobs in the three industries covered are nonexistent. Thus, if some sort of composite measure is needed, each of the occupations is perhaps best given equal weight. Such a composite index should provide an approximation to an overall comparison of real wage levels or take-home pay in modern manufacturing among the LAFTA countries.

Such an overall measure of intercountry wage differentials is presented in table 6-12. The index is an unweighted geometric formulation with the observations being the occupational indices just discussed.

As expected, Mexico ranks first in the overall index, with wages about 90% above those of LAFTA. Venezuela and Uruguay follow, with the former's real wages almost 50% above the LAFTA average and the latter's about 30% above. The very high real-wage levels of Mexico might have been somewhat surprising if this had not been found to be the case in previous chapters. Venezuela's position would be expected to be higher by most informed observers. The Uruguayan position is also somewhat intriguing, but it can be easily comprehended once the very high purchasing power of the Uruguayan peso, relative to the other LAFTA currencies, is

Table 6-12. Index of real wages in the overall industrial
sample, November 1966
(LAFTA average = 100)

Country	Index	Rank
Argentina	84	(6)
Bolivia	39	(11)
Brazil	53	(10)
Chile	97	(4)
Colombia	83	(7)
Ecuador	62	(9)
Mexico	192	(1)
Paraguay	74	(8)
Peru	94	(5)
Uruguay	131	(3)
Venezuela	148	(2)
Coefficient of Variation	= 0.45	

taken into consideration.[2] It should be noted that these results reflect the situation at the end of 1966 and conditions probably have changed since then.

The low ranking countries once more reflect conditions which are generally consistent with previous results. Bolivia is the country with lowest real wages overall, 60% below the LAFTA average. Brazil and Ecuador appear to have wage levels that are higher than those of Bolivia but still, respectively, 47% and 38% below the LAFTA average.

The rest of the countries are bunched close together. Their wages are about 35% above those of the low wage countries. On the other hand, the high wage countries seem to have real wage levels about 80% above those of the middle income countries.

Comparison with previous results

The overall comparisons presented in chapter 4 are very similar to those in table 6-12, though there are two methodological differences. In chapter 4 the quartile values of the independent variables were weighted in the construction of the final indices, which was not done here; and in previous chapters the effect of occupation was not removed from wage variation, which was done in table 6-12.

If tables 4-11 and 6-12 are compared, it is seen that rankings at the top are the same except for Uruguay. The same thing happens if the countries ranked lowest are examined, except that Chile is replaced by Bolivia. If the countries ranked in the middle positions are considered, much agreement is also seen. If the actual index values are examined, apart from Chile and Bolivia, there are noticeable differences for Venezuela, Uruguay, Colombia, and Mexico. On the other hand, there is a remarkable closeness for the rest of the countries.

The largest discrepancy is that of Bolivia, particularly surprising in view of its estimated wage levels in the pharmaceutical industry. In no occupation does Bolivia appear to have real wage levels that place it among the middle countries. Three reasons seem to be causing this phenomenon. First, because of the smaller number of observations involved when wages are additionally classified by occupation, the size of firm variable usually does not enter significantly into the set of equations used in the calculation of country wages. When occupations are mixed, the larger degrees of free-

2. It is interesting to note that Uruguay had relatively higher wages for production workers, while Venezuela paid relatively more to clerical workers. This seemed to agree with the lower levels of education in the Venezuelan labor force when contrasted with the labor force of Uruguay, as a result of which clerical workers were scarcer in the former country in relative terms, while more abundant in the latter country.

dom available allow that variable to enter the various equations. Thus, it would appear that discrepancies between the two results may be attributed to the fact that, as only eleven occupations could be utilized for the comparisons presented in this chapter, the size of firm variable ended up not affecting the wage levels. Second, it may be that part of the wage differences detected in chapter 4 occurred in those occupations not included in the overall index presented in table 6-12. Third, the wage indices presented in chapter 4 were weighted, while the overall index shown in this chapter is unweighted.

If the different conditions under which the results presented in tables 4-11 and 6-12 are taken into consideration, then the indices would not seem to differ much (the coefficient of rank correlation between them is 0.85). This appears to suggest that adjusting for occupational variation is not required for estimating net *intercountry* wage differentials, once the basic variables tied to job content (education, experience, and responsibility in this case) have been standardized.

Of course, intercountry comparisons for each occupation, such as those presented in this chapter, are useful per se. These types of comparisons shed light on patterns of wage differentials not covered by the approaches followed in chapters 4 and 5, focusing on the occupational characteristics of the workers and presenting a more detailed picture of the wage differences among LAFTA countries. To illustrate, it becomes clear that the real wage differentials discussed previously can vary by type of work (clerical vs. production) and occupation. This enriches what has been learned about possible labor migration in LAFTA, by specifying which occupations are likely to be affected. For example, if Uruguayans migrate to Venezuela, only personnel qualified for clerical work, rather than production workers, would be likely to move.

It is important to stress that tables 6-1 to 6-11 present intercountry wage comparisons for various occupations in real terms. Such results would differ were the wages expressed in money terms. Particularly, the money wages of Argentina, Venezuela, Peru, and Brazil would be higher across the board. On the other hand the money wages of Mexico, Uruguay, and Colombia would be lower.

The results would also change significantly if labor costs (rather than real wages or take-home pay) within each particular occupation were considered, because fringe benefits, employer contributions, and deductions are quite different within LAFTA. This makes the labor costs of Chile, Argentina, Brazil, and Uruguay much higher than their money wages vis-à-vis the other LAFTA countries, consequently raising their positions in the standings.

Interoccupational comparisons in the LAFTA countries

From the data presented here, conjectural glimpses can be derived of the relative abundance or scarcity of several types of labor in particular LAFTA countries. The relative standings of a country in the various occupational groups would be similar if the markets for the various types of labor shared the same characteristics (tightness, elasticity, etc.). However, if the position of a country in one occupational group is different, it probably indicates either that the number of workers in that occupation is relatively more abundant or scarce or that conditions are different in that market for that type of labor.

For clerical employees there is general uniformity in the rankings across occupational groups, as noted earlier. However, two occupations seem to behave rather differently—typist and accounting clerk. Typists are paid significantly more in Ecuador and less in Peru, relative to other occupations. Because typing is usually an occupation in which competition operates rather freely, a relative abundance of typists in Peru, and scarcity in Ecuador, would seem to be the best explanation of this finding.

Accounting clerks probably constitute the most skilled employees in the sample of key clerical occupations. Again, the market for this particular skill is generally free. In both Brazil and Argentina, accounting clerks have remunerations that are higher than expected when compared with the other clerical employees. The opposite is the case in Peru and Colombia. Thus the latter countries might be better endowed with this kind of skill, in contrast with Brazil and Argentina.

From the previous tables it can also be discerned that the wages of clerical workers in Argentina are low compared with those of production workers.[3] This may be due to the fact that Argentina has probably the most advanced educational system within LAFTA and thus turns out the relatively largest number of potential white-collar workers. Another reason may be the unions, which have been more successful and stronger in blue-collar occupations. Argentina has perhaps the strongest labor unions in LAFTA.[4]

Among the various positions considered, the production workers had a similar high degree of overall consistency. However, in two cases the standings vary substantially from those common to production workers in general. For truck drivers in Brazil and Ecuador, relative wage rates are higher, while being lower for Colombia and Argentina. These contrasts are probably determined by both market and institutional forces. Important are

3. The same is also true in the case of Uruguay.
4. This would also explain the high Argentinian rankings for production workers.

the rate of pay of drivers in the public transportation system and the strength of the unions, as well as the type of government control over the transportation network.

The other case is that of foremen, whose wages are relatively low in Argentina and high in Chile. Here it would appear that the relative abundance of secondary school graduates with the capacity for supervisory activities is probably an important determinant of the low wages in Argentina. Another important factor is that the industrial process in Argentina is more advanced than in Chile.

Production workers are more highly paid in relative terms in Argentina, the opposite of what was encountered for clerical workers. The same influencing factors are again operative—the strongest union influence in LAFTA and a probable relative shortage in the supply of blue-collar workers— causing the relatively higher wage levels for production workers.

Finally, the opposite case is visible if the LAFTA standings of clerical workers and production workers are compared with Chile's. Relatively, production workers seem to be worse off than in other LAFTA countries, especially Argentina and Uruguay. However, foremen seem to be better off in Chile, possibly because the educational system may be especially suited for supplying skilled and semi-skilled production workers. The Chilean system is probably the most developed in LAFTA after the Argentinian and Uruguayan ones, graduating relatively large proportions of primary and secondary school students, who are best suited to reach the higher positions in the spectrum of blue-collar workers.[5] The fact that demand for such workers is not as large in Chile as in the industrial sector of Argentina, also contributes to the relatively low wages of blue-collar workers in Chile.[6]

5. On this, see Marsha Goldfarb, "Some Evidence on Educational Relationships in Chile" in *Cuadernos de Economía* (Universidad Católica de Chile, 1974).

6. Another factor that could have been considered is the impact of labor unions. However, it does not seem that unions were weaker in Chile during those years, compared with the average LAFTA country.

Chapter 7. Manufacturing wages in Colombia by Francisco J. Ortega

This chapter discusses wage structure in several manufacturing industries and cities in Colombia in greater detail than in the preceding international comparisons. The methodology used was explained in chapter 2. Since many decisions on data collection were based primarily on the needs of the international analysis, the coverage of this study is limited by the definitions and choices outlined in those chapters.

The size of the sample and its distribution by industries and cities appears in table 7-1. Three main industries—textiles, pharmaceuticals, and metallurgy—were chosen for the analysis of wage differentials in Colombia. The firms in these three industries were, with few exceptions, located in Medellín, Bogotá, and Barranquilla. The sample was not geographically balanced; the textile industry being concentrated in Medellín, the pharmaceutical industry in Bogotá, and the metallurgical industry split between the two. The data in the survey were obtained by direct interviews with each firm's personnel head or industrial relations office.[1] Analysis of variance was used to check whether differences in wage variation in occupations, industries, and cities were due to sampling problems. The results were generally satisfactory, except for the occupations of lathe operator and invoice clerk.

General considerations on wage structure

The comparative analysis of wage differentials was done on three levels: by occupations, industries, and cities. All possible cross comparisons were

NOTE: The author presently is manager of the Colombian Central Bank. When this chapter was written he was the director of the Centro de Desarrollo Económico (CEDE) of the Universidad de los Andes in Colombia. He would like to convey his appreciation for the valuable contributions made by Rafael Prieto, Peter Knight, and Alvaro Reyes; for the typing done with special dedication by Mrs. Miriam de Pinzón; and for Jorge Sapoznicow's help in the statistical calculations.

1. The data collection was carried out by Roberto Martínez, a junior economist at CEDE, under the direction of Dr. Miguel Urrutia.

Table 7-1. Colombia: Size and distribution of firms by
industry and city

Industry	Total	Bogotá	Medellín	Barranquilla	Other cities[a]
Textiles	12	2	6	1	3
Pharmaceutical	8	8	–	–	–
Metallurgy	10	4	4	1	1
Subtotal	30	14	10	2	4
Other[b]	8	3	–	2	3
Total	38	17	10	4	7

[a]Cartagena, Las Flores, and Cajica; Itagui and Envigado are included in other industries.
[b]Glass, tires, and beer.

not always made due to data limitations. For instance, comparison among
occupations was undertaken only at the industry level. No comparisons
were made of wage payments for different industries and cities for the same
occupation. In some cases, subdivisions were made according to type of
occupation (clerical or production).

In general, the pattern of wage differentials varies according to the state
of development in each country. In countries where agriculture is the pre-
dominant economic activity, wage differentials will be small due to lack of
employment opportunities outside the agricultural sector, a narrower set of
jobs and occupations, and the low general educational level of the labor
force.

With increasing industrialization, wage differentials widen considerably
because of the establishment of new industries and new occupations, the
demand for new skills, and the improvement of education.[2] Colombia fits
this last case. It has an agricultural sector absorbing a high percentage of
the labor force, with industry developed to the stage of durable goods
production.

As development becomes more established and industry acquires greater
predominance, wage differentials diminish. This tendency is evident in the
more advanced countries of Europe and in the United States, especially in
occupational and interindustrial differentials, although it is less marked
among regions and sexes.[3]

2. Lloyd G. Reynolds and Cynthia H. Taft, *The Evolution of Wage Structure* (New Haven,
Conn.: Yale University Press, 1956), p. 355; Walter Galenson, ed., *Labor in Developing
Economies* (Berkeley and Los Angeles: University of California Press, 1962); Clark Kerr et
al., *Industrialism and Industrial Man* (Cambridge, Mass: Harvard University Press, 1960).
3. See Reynolds and Taft, *Evolution of Wage Structure*, p. 359; Paul G. Keat, "Long-run

In the 1960s, Colombia had high rates of unemployment, fluctuating between 12% and 18% of the urban labor force, with the greatest incidence among women and the young.[4] Unemployment was mainly structural, and in spite of efforts to increase the demand for labor, it remains high due to the growing labor supply in urban centers.

The presence of high unemployment coincides with pronounced wage differentials. Due to industrialization, new jobs demand special technical requirements, and their wages vary considerably because of abnormal labor market conditions. Such unemployment appears to contribute to high differentials. First, it has been found that if unemployment is low there is a tendency for the wage structure to compress under the effects of an increase in the demand for labor. Just the opposite occurs in periods of high unemployment.[5] Second, the excess of manpower above requirements results in the semi-artificial creation of a large range of unskilled or semi-skilled occupations, particularly in the service sector, which tends to enlarge the differentials.

Wage differentials by occupation

This subject is quite familiar in the literature, reflecting the interest of governments, trade unions, labor economists, and others. Questions about the size of occupational wage differentials, their causes and their historical trends, have been repeatedly explored. In Colombia, quantifications of these differentials appear to be of first priority.

Table 7-2 presents an index of skilled to unskilled wage differentials by industry, using the average wages for janitor as base. Fundamentally, the method explained in Perlman and in the studies by Ober and Kanninen is followed.[6]

Eleven occupations were included in the index, those having the most precise definition and a large number of observations (the key occupations). For this reason, and also because the index is not so useful for a

Changes in Occupational Wage Structure, 1900–1956," *Journal of Political Economy* 68 (December 1960), p. 590; Richard Perlman, "Forces Widening Occupational Wage Differentials," *Review of Economics and Statistics* 40 (May 1958), p. 107.

4. Francisco J. Ortega and Rafael Isaza, *Urban Surveys in Employment and Unemployment,* monograph no. 29 (Bogotá: Centro de Estudios de Desarrollo Económico [CEDE], 1969), p. 113.

5. Reynolds and Taft, *Evolution of Wage Structure;* Melvin W. Reder, *Labor in a Growing Economy* (New York: Wiley, 1958).

6. Perlman, "Forces Widening Occupational Wage Differentials," p. 107; Harry Ober, "Occupational Wage Differentials, 1907–1947," *Monthly Labor Review* 71 (August 1948); Toivo Kanninen, "Occupational Wage Relationships in Manufacturing," *Monthly Labor Review* 76 (November 1953).

Table 7-2. Colombia: Skilled and unskilled wage differentials by
occupation and industry with janitor as base, November 1966

Occupation	Industry		
	Textile	Metallurgy	Pharmaceutical
Production			
Janitor	100	100	100
Foreman	201	200	200
Truck driver	145	146	149
Machine operator	125	132	158
Lathe operator	171	162	273
Maintenance			
electrician	159	156	244
Quality controller	147	162	-
Clerical			
File clerk	210	208	199
Typist	164	181	207
Invoice clerk	252	290	244
Accounting clerk	269	230	228
Cashier	361	514	302

wide range of occupations, the better paid occupations in the sample were
excluded. Occupations were divided into two groups, those in production
and those in clerical work.

The indices in table 7-2 show similar variations among industries, particularly for textile and metallurgy. The occupations of foreman and truck
driver hardly differ among industries, but show differences of 100% and
nearly 50%, respectively, in relation to the base occupation. The substantial wage differentials are usually very similar among the three industries.
In all industries, janitor is the lowest paid occupation.

The other production occupations have similar wage differentials for the
textile and metallurgical industries, but not for the pharmaceutical industry, where far higher levels for electrician, lathe operator, and operator of
industrial machines are observed.[7] In the first two industries, the following
order of differentials is given ranging from smallest to largest: operator of
industrial machine, truck driver, maintenance electrician, quality control-

7. For lathe operators, analysis of variance suggested that sampling problems might be
affecting the results obtained.

ler, lathe operator, and foreman. This order appears to indicate a certain correlation between higher qualifications and increasing wage differentials.

To summarize, high differentials are found among these production occupations, reaching to about twice the base level. The pharmaceutical industry, which differs from the others, only includes firms located in Bogotá, which may partly explain such differences.

The group of clerical occupations shows two special characteristics: considerable similarity in the occupational indices among industries, and generally more marked differentials between occupations than in the base of production positions. The latter is basically due to the high index number for cashier in each industry.

With minor exceptions, there are similar differentials among industries. Typist and file clerk are the lowest of the clerical group, with differentials between 64% and 110% above the base occupation of janitor. The invoice and accounting clerks are in the middle with differences reaching 2.5 times the base wage. Cashier has the largest variation between industries and an average wage more than three times greater than the base occupation.

The main finding of the wage comparison by occupation is the existence of wide differences among occupations, and contrastingly similar differentials between industries, especially in textiles and metallurgy. As previously indicated, occupational wage differences will be affected by the stage of industrialization in the country and by variations in the qualitative composition of the labor force, such as education and experience.

Relation between wages and the qualitative factors

To analyze the impact of factors like education, experience, and responsibility on wage differentials, the logarithms of wages were regressed against education, experience, and initiative for each industry and by groups of clerical and plant occupations. The results are shown in table 7-3.[8]

The coefficients of determination were always significantly different from zero at a 0.01 level of significance. The three variables explain 50% or more of the total variation in every case, which is satisfactory. Education, experience, and responsibility are positively associated with wages. In all cases the most important explanatory variable is education, followed by responsibility. The regression coefficients for both are significant at the 0.01 level, the only exception being that of production occupations in the pharmaceutical industry.

Experience is significant in only two regressions. This seems to indicate

8. The regressions covered more occupations than appear in table 7-2, as they refer to the total sample.

Table 7-3. Colombia: Results of various regression experiments[a]

Occupation	Regression coefficient			Coefficient of determination (R^2)	Constant
	Educ.	Exp.	Resp.		
Production					
Textile	.1656 (.0346)	.0192[b] (.0441)	.1573 (.0462)	0.62	0.9671
Metallurgy	.2466 (.0384)	-.0499[b] (.0434)	-.0859 (.0470)	0.56	1.0077
Pharmaceutical	.3151 (.0379)	-.0218[b] (.0403)	.0394[b] (.0396)	0.79	0.9632
Clerical					
Textile	.1954 (.0503)	.0203[b] (.0467)	.2682 (.0399)	0.72	0.9190
Metallurgy	.2 (.0597)	.1380 (.0562)	.2036 (.0431)	0.73	0.5192
Pharmaceutical	.2801 (.0767)	.1288 (.0177)	.1227 (.0519)	0.59	0.3448
All occupations					
Textile	.2432 (.0304)	.0470[b] (.0358)	.1660 (.0322)	0.65	0.7000
Metallurgy	.3138 (.0363)	.0765[b] (.0406)	.0995 (.0363)	0.60	0.4999
Pharmaceutical	.2952 (.0358)	.0556[b] (.0394)	.0840 (.0325)	0.75	0.6767

[a]The function was log w = a + bEduc. + cExp. + dResp.
[b]Not significantly different from zero at 0.10 level.

that experience (measured in years) does not strongly influence the wage level, implying the probable importance of on the job training to the entrepreneur, possibly because technological requirements are new or changing, and thus prior training is irrelevant.[9]

As previously reported in using the skilled-unskilled wage index, similar results were found within each industry. A parallel situation emerges from the regression analysis, since the coefficients of determination are alike, especially for textiles and metallurgy. All these results indicate that an organized labor market exists, that the three principal industries pay higher

9. Nevertheless, results for this variable have to be examined carefully for definitional problems and estimation difficulties. For example, the variable could have been confused by some employers with seniority. In addition, there are indications of some multicollinearity between experience and the other independent variables.

wages for better work qualifications, and that competition influences wages in each of them.

Interindustry wage differentials for the same occupation

Since the chosen industries and firms are among the most developed in the country, with modern administrative methods and wage policies, it might be expected that wage differentials amongst them would be small, especially for simple and comparable occupations. This would be especially so given the use of the same wage concept in the calculations. On the other hand, it is known that large differences may not only occur between occupations, but also within occupations.

The comparison of differentials for each occupation between industries is made by measuring the relative dispersion of wages by means of coefficients of variation. For a particular industry, the coefficient of variation measures the relative dispersion of the salaries among the firms that comprise the industry. An effort was made to measure wage differentials also by running regressions at the occupational level. Unfortunately, probably as a consequence of the small number of observations in each occupation and the narrow range of variation in the independent variables, the results were not satisfactory.

To begin with, the degree of wage variation is considered. Table 7-4 gives, for each industry, the relative dispersion of wages between firms. The intraindustry coefficients of variation do not appear to be that much different for each of the clerical and production occupations considered. This is especially so if the occupations which came out suspect in the analysis of variance testing for sampling problems (invoice clerk and lathe operator), as well as those having few observations per industry (machine operator and file clerk), are excluded.

The following additional points are evident from an examination of the results in table 7-4:

1. The coefficient of variation ranges from 0.13 to 0.35 if the occupations just cited are taken out.

2. The average coefficient of variation is 0.25 for textiles, 0.24 for metallurgy, and 0.27 for pharmaceuticals, which means that wages for each occupation vary on the average by 25% of the mean wage, a high rate of variation overall.

3. The pharmaceutical industry differs significantly from the other two industries mainly in the occupations of maintenance electrician, machine operator, lathe operator, invoice clerk, and file clerk. This industry shows more dispersion than the others.

4. The textile and metallurgical industries generally have very similar

Table 7-4. Colombia: Coefficients of variation in wages classified
by occupation and industry, November 1966

Occupation	Industry		
	Textile	Metallurgy	Pharmaceutical
Production			
Janitor	.25	.26	.18
Foreman	.31	.18	.30
Truck driver	.21	.15	.17
Machine operator	.22	.23	.52
Lathe operator	.16	.16	.34
Maintenance			
electrician	.13	.18	.30
Quality controller	.34	.31	-
Clerical			
File clerk	.21	.25	.11
Typist	.24	.22	.27
Invoice clerk	.47	.45	.15
Accounting clerk	.29	.34	.35
Cashier	.34	.30	.26

coefficients of variation. For production occupations the dispersion is usually greater in textiles (0.24) than in metallurgy (0.21).

5. The degree of relative wage variation among industries and firms,
combined with high values in the skilled-unskilled worker index, indicates
considerable wage differences in Colombia, both within and between occupations.

The similarities in the skilled-unskilled indexes across industries reveal a
definite pattern of interoccupational differentials. They suggest that differentials between occupations are determined by market forces and that
they reflect workers' qualifications. On the other hand, the relatively high
coefficients of wage variation in specific occupations suggest that, within
occupations, institutional effects (e.g., employer's preferences and labor
union strength) predominate. This means that market forces determine the
wage range for specific occupations, but that institutional factors determine
the actual wage rate paid. These results are consistent with other findings.[10]

10. For example: "It was demonstrated that, in modern large scale industry, all wage rates
are administered wage rates; and that the influence of economic forces is mediated through
administrative decisions rather than expressed directly in the market place. It was also as-

Wage comparisons between industries for all occupations combined

It has been maintained that high wages tend to be paid in those industries which produce durable goods, in industries where large firms predominate and where there are relatively large amounts of capital per worker.[11]

Also, high wage industries seem to be located in large cities. However, there still is no satisfactory theory explaining wage differences between industries, and little empirical work has been done to test such hypotheses.

The comparison of wages with equal qualitative job content, as defined by education, experience, and responsibility, was made for the three industries first and then for the various occupational groups within them.[12] In general, the methodology used is the one described in chapter 2. Table 7-5 gives the estimated wages resulting from the application of the regression method previously discussed.

As expected, there are small interindustry differences when all occupations are considered. If clerical and production positions are combined, pharmaceuticals and metallurgy show virtually the same salary, while the textile industry is about 4% below the others. Thus, there is considerable similarity in the wages paid by these three industries after standardization by job content.[13]

By occupational groups, clerical occupations always have higher wage levels than production positions, consistent with previous findings. The textile industry is in the middle in terms of wage levels in each occupational group. The metallurgical industry has the extreme wage disparities between the clerical and production occupations, paying the highest salaries in the first case and the lowest in the second. The pharmaceutical industry has the lowest divergence between clerical and production occupations, with opposite rankings—lowest in clerical and highest in production positions.

The similarity between industries is less within the clerical and production occupations than when all occupations are grouped together. There is a

---

serted with a good show of evidence that, in many situations, economic forces determine only a range of possible wage rates rather than a specific wage rate. The location of the actual wage within this range will be influenced by custom, conventional yardsticks, management preferences and judgements, trade union pressures, and government wage relations." Reynolds and Taft, *Evolution of Wage Structure*, p.1.

11. Reder, *Labor in a Growing Economy*, pp. 357–58.

12. Responsibility proved to have no significant effect on wages, and was dropped from the equations serving as the basis for table 7-5.

13. The differences among industries are wider if simple wage averages, for all occupations, are compared before standardization.

Table 7-5. Colombia: Estimated hourly wages by industries and
occupational groups, November 1966[a]
(in pesos)

Industry	Group		Total
	Clerical	Production	
Textiles	17.48	9.36	12.75
Metallurgy	19.31	8.91[b]	13.22
Pharmaceuticals	15.72	10.67[b]	13.18

[a]Wages were estimated according to the function log w = a + bEduc. + dResp.
[b]Responsibility was not significant at the 0.10 level.

range of 3.59 pesos in clerical positions, that is, a difference somewhat
below 20%. For the production group the range is 1.76 pesos, which is a bit
lower in percentage.[14]

The metallurgical industry paid the highest wages for total and clerical
occupations. A probable explanation for this is the newness of this industry
at that time and, perhaps, higher capital-labor ratios and firm size. The
textile industry showed the lowest wages after adjustment for qualitative
requirements, consistent with expectations, as this industry is the most traditional of the three.

Wage comparisons among cities for all occupations combined

Another type of wage comparison in which the qualitative requirements
were homogenized involves the determination of the intercity wage differentials among Bogotá, Barranquilla, Medellín, and the "other cities"
listed in table 7-1. The estimated wages by city and occupational group
presented in table 7-6, suggest considerable disparity if both clerical and
production occupations are combined. The highest average wages were
paid in Medellín and Bogotá. These two cities stand apart from the others
by virtue of the relatively high wages paid. Barranquilla and the "other
cities" had much lower wages.

Such wage differences between Bogotá and Medellín and the rest of the
cities seem reasonable. However, the higher level of wages in Medellín,
when compared with Bogotá, appear unusual. It may be what Medellín
required to attract labor away from Bogotá.

Medellín paid the highest wages for both occupational groups. Compared with Bogotá, there are considerable differences between the two cities in the wages for clerical occupations, and very slight differences in the

14. In November 1966 the official exchange rate was 13.5 Colombian pesos per dollar.

Table 7-6. Colombia: Estimated hourly wages by cities
and occupational groups, November 1966[a]
(in pesos)

| City | Group | | Total |
	Clerical	Production	
Bogotà	16.24	10.13	13.28
Barranquilla	12.23[b]	7.10[b]	9.03[b]
Medellín	19.91	10.26	14.71
Other cities	15.12	7.62	9.95

[a]Wages were estimated according to the function log w = a + bEduc. + dResp.
[b]Responsibility was not significant at the 0.10 level.

Table 7-7. Colombia: Estimated hourly wages by cities
and industries, November 1966[a]
(in pesos)

| City | Industry | | |
	Textiles	Metallurgy	Pharmaceuticals
Bogotà	13.40	12.87	12.90
Barranquilla	13.27	6.61[b]	-
Medellín	14.66	16.56	-
Other cities	9.14	11.50	-

[a]Wages were estimated according to the function log w = a + bEduc. + dResp.
[b]Only education was significant at the 0.10 level.

wages for production occupations. Barranquilla and the "other cities" show similar wages in production positions. For clerical occupations, the wages paid in Barranquilla were even lower in relative terms compared with those paid in "other cities", the divergence being substantial.

Wage comparisons by city and industry

Table 7-7 presents the results of the wage comparisons cross-classified by city and industry. This could not be done for the pharmaceutical industry since all firms were located in Bogotá.

Table 7-7 shows that the estimated wages corresponding to the textile industry were practically the same in Bogotá, Barranquilla, and Medellín. Medellín's higher wage levels are corroborated by the industry classification, but the city's position relative to the other cities appears to be lower than what emerged from the occupational group comparison. Likewise, Barranquilla, which in the former table showed lower levels than other cities for clerical as well as production occupations, is now close to Bogotá in wages paid in the textile industry. The group of "other cities" had a lower wage level compared with Medellín, Bogotá, and Barranquilla. The difference between Medellín and the "other cities" group was approximately 50%.

There are greater relative differences among the various cities in the metallurgical industry. Medellín is the city with highest wages in this industry, 28% above those of Bogotá, and 44% higher than in the "other cities." The wages in Barranquilla are very low in relative terms in this industry. However, this may be influenced by the small number of observations in the metallurgical industry in this city.

Finally, as an overall view of the dispersion of estimated wages by industry, their coefficients of variation were estimated (table 7-8). Furthermore, these were also calculated for the various occupational groups within each industry. Wages in clerical occupations, it was found, vary less than those of production occupations, with the textile and pharmaceutical industries having the least variation in these positions (coefficient of variation = 0.18).

For production occupations the least dispersed wages were in metallurgy, but the coefficients in the other two industries were only slightly higher (0.02 points). For all occupations combined, the pharmaceutical industry showed the smaller dispersion, followed by the textile industry.

General conclusions

The main findings of this chapter are the following:

1. Appreciable wage differences were observed between occupations up to three times the base in production occupations and five times in clerical occupations.

2. In each industry and occupational group there is a high correlation between wages and education and responsibility—but not experience. This suggests that market forces determine a wage scale varying with job con-

Table 7-8. Colombia: Coefficients of variation in
estimated wages by industry and occupational groups,
November 1966

Industry	Group		Total
	Clerical	Production	
Textiles	0.18	0.26	0.32
Metallurgy	0.20	0.24	0.35
Pharmaceuticals	0.18	0.26	0.24

tent or worker's qualifications and that employers train new workers on the job.

3. The dispersion of wages among firms for each occupation was quite high, averaging about 25% of the mean. This suggests that strong elements of market imperfection and institutional factors determine the wage rates for the same occupation in the various firms.

4. The comparisons of standardized wages by industry, city, and occupational group brought out the following points:

(a) There are similar wage levels among industries, when all occupations are combined (table 7-5), and among cities with regard to the textile industry (table 7-7).

(b) There are important differences among clerical and production wages in each industry and city (table 7-5 and 7-6).

(c) According to cities, wages range from highest to lowest in the following order: Medellín, Bogotá, the group of "other cities," and Barranquilla.

Chapter 8. Manufacturing wage differentials in Venezuela and Uruguay
by Juan J. Buttari

The primary objective of this chapter is to measure wage differentials in nine industries of the Venezuelan manufacturing sector and in four manufacturing industries in Uruguay. It also attempts to (a) test the consistency of the results with various hypotheses on the nature and type of wage differentials in developing countries, and (b) determine the relative ability of various variables to explain the dispersion of wage rates.

The chapter contains three main sections. Following a few methodological comments in this introduction, the first and second sections present and discuss wage differentials in the Venezuelan and Uruguayan manufacturing sectors, respectively. The third section compares aspects of the labor markets in both countries and suggests policy guidelines.

The methodology used is similar to that employed in previous chapters measuring intercountry and national differentials. The measurement of the wage structure is accomplished on two levels: in the first, differentials not adjusted for worker's skills are measured; in the second, regression methods are used to adjust for these skills. Minimum wages are used instead of average rates. The former are preferable because there are skill grades in any given occupation. In developing countries "the distribution of skills . . . is probably skewed heavily to the low side within any classification."

NOTE: The author is grateful to colleagues on the staffs of the Instituto de Investigaciones Económicas, Universidad Católica Andrés Bello (Venezuela), and of the Facultad de Ciencias Económicas y de Administración, Universidad de la República (Uruguay), for their efforts in collecting and processing the data used in this study. These tasks were supervised in Venezuela by Mr. Jose Ignacio Rodríguez assisted by Mr. Luis Lange and, in Uruguay, by Mr. Raul Vigorito. Messrs. Denisard Alves, John R. Eriksson, Robert Ferber, Stephan MacGaughey, Joseph Grunwald, Ricardo Martínez, Philip Musgrove, Jorge Salazar-Carrillo, Joseph Tryon, and an anonymous referee offered helpful comments. Mr. Jeffrey Schott and Miss Lois Dublin provided needed editorial assistance. Mr. Schott also provided valuable research assistance. The author is indebted to Mr. Joseph Tu and Ms. Marcia Mason for their assistance in the use of various computer programs.

Given this state of affairs, the use of average wage rates "underestimates the true premium for skill in the less developed countries."[1]

Firms were classified according to national origin of the equity capital into the following groups: totally national, predominantly national, predominantly foreign, and of equal shares (capital is 50% national and 50% foreign). This classification allows an estimate to be made of the differential effect upon wages of the firm's sources of capital. The Uruguayan sample was collected in the area of Montevideo while the Venezuelan sample consists of observations from the area of Caracas and other nearby cities, like Valencia. Accordingly, some of the differentials in Venezuela might reflect geographical effects. In both countries the industries surveyed constituted a subsector of substantial and increasing importance within manufacturing. Hence, their wage structures are probably representative of that corresponding to the overall manufacturing sectors.

Venezuela

The social setting

Compared to the situation in the early 1900s Venezuelan society by the 1960s had evolved into a relatively fluid community. Social mobility was significant and entrepreneurial dynamism played an important social and economic role. Nevertheless, in spite of these achievements, the society still faced some pressing problems. The number of young people entering the labor force each year for the first time was about twice the number of new jobs being created, and as would be expected, the highest rate of unemployment was among young workers. In 1971, for example, 70% of the unemployed were between 15 and 29 years old.[2]

From 1950–60 the gross domestic product (GDP) grew at an annual compound rate of 9.3% while industrial gross domestic product (IGDP) grew at the rate of 13.2%.[3] Both growth rates fell from 1960–66: GDP grew at the rate of 4.9% while IGDP grew at 9.0%. Nevertheless, if the industrialization process is measured by the ratio of the rate of growth of IGDP to that of GDP, this process grew at a faster rate during 1960–66 than from 1950–60.

From 1950–66 the industrial sector provided employment for 12% to

1. Elliot J. Berg, "Wage Structures in Less Developed Countries" in *Wage Policy Issues in Economic Development,* ed. Anthony D. Smith (London: MacMillan, 1969; New York: St. Martin's Press, 1969), pp. 301-02.

2. Organization of American States, *El Esfuerzo Interno y las Necesidades de Financiamiento Externo para el Desarrollo de Venezuela,* CIAP 568, vol. 1 (August 1972), p. 50.

3. Organization of American States, *El Esfuerzo y las Necesidades de Financiamiento Externo para el Desarrollo de Venezuela,* CIAP 489, add. 1 (May 1971), p. 78.

13% of the employed labor force without significant changes during any subperiod.[4] The stability of the rate of employment in the industrial sector in spite of the fact that IGDP grew at a faster rate than GDP probably reflects the intensive use of labor saving technologies in the industrial sector.

It has been suggested that expanding industries tend to raise wages at a faster rate than other industries.[5] The rates of growth of value added and of employment originating in the surveyed industries during the 1960–66 period, and the 1963–66 and 1965–66 subperiods, indicate that during these periods the most dynamic industries were household appliances and automobile assembly and the least dynamic were textiles and rubber products.

In terms of their dynamism, metallurgy, pharmaceuticals, and vegetable oils occupy a medium to high position, while paper-cellulose and cement fall in a medium to low level.[6] On the basis of this evidence, the hypothesis enunciated at the beginning of this paragraph leads one to infer that household appliances, automobile assembly, metallurgy, pharmaceuticals, and vegetable oils can be expected to be high or medium to high paying industries while paper, cement, textiles, and rubber products can be expected to be low or medium to low paying industries.

The Venezuelan sample

The nine industries represented in the Venezuelan sample, with their main products, are as follows:

Industry	*Products*
Textiles	Shirts, linen, etc.
Pharmaceuticals	Drugs and vitamins
Metallurgy	Metal pipes, water tanks, etc.
Automobile assembly	Automobile and truck assembly
Cement	Cement, clay, etc.
Rubber	Tires and other rubber products
Vegetable oils	Oils, butter, margarine
Paper	Paper, paper bags, cardboard, etc.
Household appliances	Electric household appliances

4. Based on Banco Interamericano de Desarrollo, Venezuela 1950–67: Variables, Parametros y Metodologia de las Cuentas Nacionales, table 9 (División de Desarrollo Económico y Social, December 1968).

5. See, for example, John T. Dunlop, "Productivity and the Wage Structure" in *Income, Employment, and Public Policy, Essays in Honor of A. E. Hanson,* ed. Lloyd A. Metzler (New York: W. W. Norton, 1948), pp. 341–62; Berg, "Wage Structures," p. 296.

6. Based on data provided by CORDIPLAN, the central planning agency, and from data in Organization of American States, *El Esfuerzo y las Necesidades,* pp. 80–84. The data correspond to industries which are generally more comprehensive than the industries sampled.

Table 8-1. Venezuela: Sample composition by industry, number of observations, and origin of capital

Industry	Individual observations	Firms	Nature of capital				
			Totally national	Predominantly national	Predominantly foreign	Totally foreign	Equal shares
Textiles	50	3[a]	2	-	-	-	-
Pharmaceuticals	138	9[a]	3	-	-	5	-
Metallurgy	78	6[a]	5	-	-	-	-
Automobile assembly	45	3	1	-	-	2	-
Cement	25	2	1	1	-	-	-
Rubber	52	3	-	-	2	-	1
Vegetable oil	54	3	2	1	-	-	-
Paper	50	3	2	-	1	-	-
Household appliances	62	4	2	-	2	-	-
Total	554	36	18	2	5	7	1

[a]The national origin of the capital in one firm is unspecified.

Table 8-1 shows the number of firms sampled, the number of wage observations in each industry, and the distribution of firms by origin of capital. The sample consists of 554 wage observations of which 353 (nearly 64%) correspond to key occupations.

Wage differentials unadjusted for worker skills

Measuring wage differentials without explicitly adjusting by worker skills permits the determination of the change caused in the wage structure when adjustment for these skills is made later on. Table 8-2 presents interindustry differentials by occupational category for key occupations. It reveals some similarities and contrasts between the interindustry ranks and indexes corresponding to clerical occupations (column 1) and to production occupations (column 2).

The main contrasts in the industry indexes and ranks are that (1) the interindustry range for clerical occupations is considerably smaller than for production occupations and (2) all industry ranks change in moving from one category to another, except in the case of pharmaceuticals.

The relatively small interindustry dispersion shown within clerical occupations suggests the existence, in the market for clerical personnel, of a better information system than for production personnel, and relatively few market imperfections. Another explanation might be that clerical occupations are more homogeneous. However, as these results refer to occupations specified in detail, and common to all firms and industries surveyed, this alternative explanation seems less likely.

Classifying the industries surveyed as high paying, low paying, and intermediate according to minimum wages, the following array is obtained:[7]

High paying: Vegetable oils, Pharmaceutical, Metallurgy.

Paying intermediate rates: Rubber, Automobile assembly.

Low paying: Paper, Cement, Textiles.

In the literature, producers of "hard durable" goods have been identified as "high wage" in contrast to manufacturers of "soft" goods (e.g., textiles and clothing) which are deemed "notoriously low wage payers." A rationale for the distinction is that industries producing durable goods tend to be more unstable over the business cycle and, consequently, have to pay higher wages to offset long periods of unemployment.[8]

---

7. Electric products show no definite pattern. Differences in definitions and coverage make it difficult to compare these results with those obtained by Haydee Castillo and Manuel Rodríguez Trujillo in *El Costo de la Mano de Obra en Venezuela en Relación a América Latina* (Caracas: Empresas Mendoza, 1965).

8. Melvin W. Reder, *Labor in a Growing Economy*, (New York: Wiley, 1958), pp. 361–

Accordingly, metallurgy is usually classified as a high paying industry, while textiles is frequently cited as an example of a typically low paying industry.[9] In respect to minimum wage, the evidence thus far presented in this study tends to support this practice.[10]

A hypothesis was postulated in a previous section of a direct correspondence between rate of growth and industry ranking according to wage rates—that those with the highest growth rates would pay relatively high wage rates. A look at the array presented here reveals a positive although imperfect correspondence with this hypothesis. The automobile industry, one of the two most dynamic industries, occupied an intermediate position while the relative position of electric household appliances, the other most dynamic industry, was indeterminate. One plausible explanation of the "irregular" standing of automobile assembly might be the relatively low level of skills required by assembly operations and the relative abundance of such labor. To a lesser extent, this explanation might be applicable also to electric appliances.

These somewhat ambiguous results suggest that the effect of the rate of growth upon wage rates varies with occupation.[11] A perusal of the industry ranks and indexes at each occupational category tended to corroborate this second hypothesis. The correspondence between industry performance and wage rate indexes seemed stronger for production than for clerical occupations. Thus, for example, when only production occupations were considered, the results for all industries but one—auto assembly—were consistent with the initial hypothesis (table 8-2). The greater mobility of clerical workers relative to production workers might explain these results. Again, this would be consistent with the hypothesis advanced earlier that a better communications system and less imperfections in the market for clerical workers might exist.

Wage dispersion among firms by industry and occupational group are shown in table 8-3.[12] It shows that (1) the wage dispersion in clerical oc-

67; and Leonard W. Weiss, "Concentration and Labor Earnings," *American Economic Review* 56 (March 1966), pp. 96–117.

9. See for example, International Labour Office, "Changing Wage Structures: An International Review," *International Labour Review* 73 (March 1956), pp. 275–83.

10. One factor tending to pull textile wages downward is that this industry traditionally employs a relatively high proportion of women. According to Venezuelan law, equal work should command equal pay irrespective of sex. However, as has been pointed out elsewhere, in Venezuela women are discriminated against. See U.S. Bureau of Labor Statistics, *Labor Law and Practice in Venezuela,* pp. 13–46.

11. These results would not be substantially different had the rates of growth corresponded to a sole period (1960–66) or subperiod (1963–66 or 1965–66).

12. The small number of firms sampled in most of the industries limits the possibility of

Table 8-2. Venezuela: Interindustry differentials and industry ranks
(Differentials not adjusted by worker's skills; textiles = 100)

| Industry | Occupational group | | | | | |
| | Clerical | | Production | | All | |
	Index	Rank	Index	Rank	Index	Rank
Textiles	100	7	100	9	100	9
Pharmaceuticals	118	2	161	2	142	2
Metallurgy	125	1	144	4	136	3
Vegetable oils	106	3	170	1	143	1
Electric products	93	9	156	3	129	4
Paper	103	6	115	8	110	8
Cement	99	8	126	7	114	7
Rubber	105	5	132	6	120	6
Automobile assembly	106	3	136	5	123	5
Interindustry range	32		70		43	

cupations, in four industries (vegetable oils, metallurgy, textiles, and cement), is substantially different to the dispersion in production occupations; (2) the traditional industries (cement and textiles) have the lowest dispersion within occupational categories, suggesting that firms within each industry experience similar wage setting processes;[13] and (3) the intraindustry dispersion seems greater within clerical occupations. This is true for seven of the nine industries, a surprising result in view of the narrow interindustry dispersion within clerical occupations. The apparent discrepancy might be due to the fact that blue-collar workers are unionized to a greater extent than white-collar workers and that blue-collar unions are more influential within a given industry. As a consequence, within industries union pressures might exert a stronger equalizing effect upon industrial wages than upon administrative wages.

Table 8-4 presents occupational wage differentials (indexes) by key occupation and industry, using the mean wage of janitor as the base. The table discloses considerable variation of the occupational indexes across industries, accompanied by substantial fluctuation in the position of each

---

attaining significant conclusions. Accordingly, few comments are possible and these should be deemed highly tentative.

13. John T. Dunlop, "The Task of Contemporary Wage Theory" in *New Concepts on Wage Determination,* ed. George W. Taylor and Frank C. Pierson (New York: McGraw Hill, 1957), p. 131.

Table 8-3. Venezuela: Industry ranking according to intraindustry wage dispersion by occupational groups and wage levels[a]

(Figures in parentheses are coefficients of variation in percent)

Rank	Occupational group		
	Clerical	Production	All
1	Vegetable oils (41.67)	Metallurgy (34.50)	Vegetable oils (33.93)
2	Paper (31.83)	Rubber (32.06)	Rubber (30.75)
3	Rubber (29.01)	Vegetable oils (28.59)	Metallurgy (28.33)
4	Electric products (28.01)	Pharmaceutical (25.79)	Pharmaceutical (26.33)
5	Pharmaceutical (27.10)	Electric products (24.86)	Electric products (26.20)
6	Automobile assembly (22.76)	Paper (20.89)	Paper (24.72)
7	Metallurgy (22.28)	Automobile assembly (17.29)	Automobile assembly (19.30)
8	Textiles (16.15)	Textiles (10.09)	Textiles (12.60)
9	Cement[b] (15.30)	Cement[b] (8.65)	Cement[b] (10.64)

[a]Intraindustry dispersion is equivalent to interfirm dispersion.
[b]Only two firms.

Table 8-4. Venezuela: Interoccupational differentials by industry
(Janitor = 100)

Occupation	Textile	Pharma-ceutical	Metallurgy	Vegetable oils	Electric products	Paper	Cement	Rubber	Automobile assembly	Mean
File clerk	118	134	273	142	97	179	190	111	169	153
Typist	129	174	185	113	125	144	184	142	137	148
Invoice clerk	170	174	150	168	137	123	173	128	210	177
Accounting clerk	156	212	256	208	221	183	166	176	240	202
Mean wage for clerical positions	193	188	244	186	148	236	203	159	214	194
Janitor	100	100	100	100	100	100	100	100	100	100
Industrial machine operator	125	101	166	132	121	173	169	156	142	141
Lathe operator	230	298	244	161	186	269	198	184	199	217
Electrician	148	254	163	184	265	255	203	162	202	204
Engineer	335	532	685	1052	581	485	608	397	647	590
Driver	143	177	166	141	173	176	194	129	242	169
Foreman	210	254	360	226	227	307	260	208	312	259
Mean wage for production positions	184	245	269	285	236	252	247	191	263	240
Overall mean	188	222	258	244	200	245	229	177	243	221

occupation relative to the others. Nevertheless, some trends are discernible. Engineers consistently have the highest wage rates while the lowest are paid to janitors. Foremen and cashiers are consistently high paid, while operators of industrial machines and typists are consistently low.

The wage differential between college graduates and unskilled workers can be approximated by the wage differential between engineer and janitor; on the average engineers earned 490% more than janitors. The wage differential between lathe operators and janitors may be used as an indicator of the skilled/unskilled differential; on the average, lathe operators earned 117% more than janitors. Both of these results are consistent with previous findings.[14] The differential between a college graduate (engineer) and an unskilled worker in Venezuela is about the same as that existing in the United States between physicians and unskilled workers, according to Kothari's estimates.[15] This would be consistent with the assertion that, in relative terms, engineers are as scarce in Venezuela as physicians are in the United States. The ratio of wages of skilled to unskilled workers is consistent with the assertion that the "wages of skilled manual workers will stand in a ratio of at least two to one with those of unskilled nonagricultural laborers in countries at early or intermediate states of industrial development."[16]

In discussions of white-collar and blue-collar wages, the differential between a typist and a skilled manual worker is often mentioned. Two skilled occupations serve for this comparison in the sample—electricians and lathe operators. The former earned wages about 37% higher than typists, while the latter earned wages about 46% higher. On the other hand, the average wage rate of a typist is only 4% higher than that of an operator of industrial machines, a semi-skilled worker. Accordingly, these results do not reflect a bias favoring clerical wages and do not support Chen, who found that white-collar workers averaged more than twice the rates of blue-collar workers.[17] Therefore, the results do not tend to support the hypothesis that

14. See H. Gunter, "Changes in Occupational Wage Differentials," *International Labour Review* 89 (February 1964), pp. 136–55; John R. Eriksson, "Wage Structures and Economic Development in Selected Latin American Countries, A Comparative Analysis" (Ph.D. diss., University of California, Berkeley, 1966), pp. 225–37; V.N. Kothari, "Disparities in Earnings among Different Countries," *Economic Journal* 80 (September 1970) pp. 605–16; Berg, "Wage Structures," pp. 298–318.

15. Kothari, "Disparities in Earnings."

16. Peter Gregory, *Industrial Wages in Chile* (Ithaca, N.Y.: Cornell University, 1967), p. 86.

17. Chi Yi Chen, *Economia Social del Trabajo* (Caracas: Universidad Católica, 1969), pp. 187–89. As no universal classification of workers by skill levels exists, this paper makes an effort to represent skill levels by occupations used in the same fashion as in other studies. See, for example, Gregory, *Industrial Wages in Chile*, pp. 86–87.

employers hold nonmanual employees in higher esteem than manual workers because the former partake in many of the employer's responsibilities.[18]

The index in table 8-4 and previous estimates by the U.S. Bureau of Labor Statistics are consistent in that clerical wage dispersion is narrower than production wage dispersion; cashiers and bookkeepers are relatively high wage occupations; foremen are the best paid skilled production workers, suggesting a premium on responsibility.[19]

Wage differentials adjusted for worker skills

The extent to which wage dispersion is explained by worker skills and by establishment variables is estimated by regressing the logarithm of minimum wages against the three independent variables that stand for worker skills and then adding, in successive steps, establishment variables. Including all the independent variables, the linearized model can be expressed as:

$$\text{In. wage} = \text{constant} + b_1 \text{ education} + b_2 \text{ experience} + b_3 \text{ responsibility} + b_4 \text{ size of firm} + b_5 \text{ industry} + b_6 \text{ firm} + b_7 \text{ occupation} + \text{random factors.}$$

Industry, firm, and occupation are measured by sets of dummy variables.

The findings of another study can be used as a frame of reference. Giora Hanoch found that in the United States personal and establishment variables together would account for about 34% of wage dispersion and that interindustry and interoccupational effects reduced unexplained variation by about 12%.[20] On the basis of a previous study, Hanoch estimated that about 30% of the variation in wages was explainable because it was due to random and transitory factors.

In the present case, when wages of all the key occupations in the Venezuelan sample are regressed against education, experience, and responsibility, about 35% of the total wage variation is accounted for. Education and responsibility have positive coefficients and are significantly different from zero at the 0.01 level. Experience, with a negative coefficient, is not significantly different from zero.

When size of firm is allowed into the regression, its coefficient is nega-

18. This is sometimes referred to as the "theory of delegated responsibility." Fritz Croner, "Salaried Employees in Modern Societies," *International Labour Review* 69 (February 1954), pp. 97–110.

19. *Labor Law and Practice in Venezuela,* pp. 46, 47, and 52.

20. See Giora Hanoch, "Personal Earnings and Investment in Schooling" (Ph.D. diss., University of Chicago, 1965), pp. 24–27, cited in Belton M. Fleisher, *Labor Economics: Theory and Evidence* (Englewood Cliffs, N.J.: Prentice Hall, 1970), pp. 211–13. The independent variables used by Hanoch were schooling, age, race, region, occupation, and industry. The data were taken from the U.S. Census of Population, 1960.

tive and significant at the 0.01 level, and $\bar{R}^2$ increases by slightly less than 2 percentage points. Introducing dummy variables for industry as a next step increases $\bar{R}^2$ by another 2 percentage points. A similar increase in $\bar{R}^2$ occurs when dummy variables representing firms are introduced as additional variables. The successive addition of these three establishment variables does not produce a substantial change in the coefficients or in the standard errors of the skill variables. Size becomes nonsignificantly different from zero at the 0.10 level when industry variables are included, which seems to indicate collinearity between size and the industry dummy variables.

A considerable increase in $\bar{R}^2$ takes place when dummy variables for occupation are included— $\bar{R}^2$ rises by 17 percentage points. At this step, responsibility remains significantly different from zero at the 0.01 level but education becomes nonsignificant. Again, this might signal the presence of collinearity between education and the occupation dummy variables and can be interpreted as suggesting that education has little effect upon wage variation within a given occupation.

A summary of the adjusted coefficient of determination is as follows:

Variables in equation	$\bar{R}^2$
Education, experience, responsibility	0.349
Education, experience, responsibility, size of firm	0.366
Education, experience, responsibility, size of firm, industry	0.390
Education, experience, responsibility, size of firm, industry, firm	0.416
Education, experience, responsibility, size of firm, industry, firm, occupation	0.585

With both skills and establishment variables included, about 59% of the dispersion of wages is explained. Considering that, as Hanoch pointed out, a significant component of the dispersion in wages is likely to reflect random and transitory factors, the model explains a relatively high proportion of explainable dispersion. Establishment variables account for about 24% of age variation, while skills account for about 35%. It would appear that responsibility is a good proxy for abilities not primarily related to formal education; the simple correlation coefficient between responsibility and education is 0.442. Experience does not seem to have any significant bearing on the dispersion of the overall wage data, and size of firm also comes out as a relatively weak variable.[21]

21. In other experiments in which administrative and industrial wages were considered separately size was able to decrease unexplained variation only by 1% to 2%. Experience always remained nonsignificantly different from zero.

IMPACT OF SKILL VARIABLES BY INDUSTRY AND OCCUPATIONAL CATEGORY

This section discusses differences in the effects of the skill variables upon wages across industries and occupational categories as revealed by regression methods. Only key occupations were considered. The equations were estimated by the use of the flexible pooling approach.[22] Size was not included in view of its low explanatory power and because it decreased the number of skill dummies that enter the equation significantly.

The model showed a higher explanatory power for production occupations than for clerical occupations; for the former $\bar{R}^2$ was 0.57, while for the latter it was only 0.30. This was due to the stronger effects of industry dummies within production occupations and reflected the greater interindustry dispersion of production wages. Where wages were regressed solely against skills $\bar{R}^2$ was 0.57 for clerical occupations, and 0.48 for production occupations, suggesting the greater influence of nonmarket forces—for example, unions—in the determination of production wages.

In two instances the sign was unexpected: first, for experience in vegetable oils, which had a negative coefficient in both occupational categories, as well as when all key occupations were pooled; and second, for responsibility in the production occupations of auto assembly, which also had a negative coefficient. Workers' responsibility showed positive coefficients when clerical occupational categories within auto assembly, as well as all key occupations, were pooled. Further experiments showed that the negative sign of workers' responsibility in key production occupations of auto assembly was due to collinearity between education and responsibility. The negative effect of workers' experience in the vegetable oil industry, though, could not be traced to multicollinearity.[23]

Experience seemed to be the least important of the three skill variables. This was suggested by the number of industries in which it entered the regression significantly, by the size of its beta coefficients relative to the coeffi-

22. Space constraints prevent the publication of the estimated equations. In no case did the entrance of a slope dummy make a previously nonsignificant skill variable significant.

23. A narrow interpretation of the negative coefficient in vegetable oils would suggest that, in this industry, workers who see their experience increased are penalized with wage reductions. This irrational result could arise from factors like hidden correlation with excluded variables. For example, age might be strongly correlated with experience. Older workers might receive relatively low wages if deemed less productive (Reder, *Labor in a Growing Economy*, p.317). If this is the case, employers will prefer younger to older workers, leaving the latter with little freedom to choose among job alternatives. This enables employers to enjoy some degree of labor exploitation (the concept is used in its non-Marxian sense). Another cause of the unexpected signs might be sex discrimination. It is possible that observations considered correspond to women with high levels of experience and initiative. As pointed out before, in Venezuela women are often discriminated against.

Table 8-5. Venezuela: Adjusted wage estimates, interindustry ranks, and interindustry indexes for grouped key occupations[a]

Industry	Key clerical occupations			Key production occupations			All key occupations		
	Wage (Bolivares)	Differential Percent	Rank	Wage (Bolivares)	Differential Percent	Rank	Wage (Bolivares)	Differential Percent	Rank
Textiles	5.75	100	(6)	4.47	100	(9)	4.93	100	(8)
Pharmacy	7.24	126	(2)	7.25	162	(1)	6.68	135	(3)
Metallurgy	6.90	120	(3)	5.80	130	(6)	5.80	118	(5)
Vegetable oils	8.65	150	(1)	7.12	159	(2)	6.89	140	(1)
Household appliances	5.75[b]	100[b]	(6)	7.09	159	(4)	6.76	137	(2)
Paper	5.75[b]	100[b]	(6)	5.21	117	(8)	4.93[b]	100[b]	(8)
Cement	5.75[b]	100[b]	(6)	5.69	127	(7)	5.63	114	(7)
Rubber	5.83	101	(5)	7.12	159	(2)	6.57	133	(4)
Automobile assembly	6.76	118	(4)	6.11	137	(5)	5.75	117	(6)
Interindustry range	50			62			40		

[a]Wages were estimated at the mean values of education, experience, and initiative and rounded to the nearest integer. Indexes are expressed in percent using the results from the textile industry as the base for comparison (i.e., textiles = 100). Size was not included in the regression model. Rank is from highest-paying to lowest-paying industries.
[b]The equation estimated for the industry did not differ significantly from textiles.

cients of the other variables, and by comparing the simple correlation of each independent variable with wages. The relatively overall weak effect of experience might be natural in a country whose manufacturing is undergoing a period of rapid expansion and modernization. In this situation employers are not interested in personnel with experience because this experience is likely to be irrelevant for the newly created jobs to be filled. A premium is placed on skills which enable employees to learn fast on the job.[24] These skills are likely to be related to the education and innate abilities of a worker rather than to his past job experience. Results suggested that the degree of difference in the impact of skill variables was smaller in clerical than in production occupations. This is consistent with the existence of smaller dispersion in interindustry wages within clerical occupations.

Table 8-5 presents estimates of industry wages and wage indexes by occupational category. The equations used to estimate the wages were analyzed in a previous subsection. The independent variables were valued at their mean values rounded to the nearest integer. Interindustry ranges showed the dispersion between the highest and lowest indexes with textile wages used as the index base.

Although industry ranks and indexes change when wages are adjusted by skills, the difference between the unadjusted and the adjusted wage structures does not seem to be great. The classification of industries according to level of payment—high, medium, and low—gives nearly the same results. Moreover, in both the adjusted and the unadjusted structures, dispersion is smaller within clerical occupations. The lack of significant differences between the unadjusted and the adjusted interindustry structures is consistent with the hypothesis that skills are uniformly distributed across industries. If so, this hypothesis would imply that due to market imperfection from differing transfer costs and / or noneconomic factors, even though there are significant interindustry wage differentials, industries are able to get similar skills for similar occcupations. Accordingly, this interference should underline the need to increase information in the labor markets and to encourage labor mobility to bring about wage differentials reflecting differences in labor skills.

To measure the origin of capital effects, experiments were made with three types of equations:[25] (1) using only an intercept dummy, (2) using only slope

24. The importance of education and training outside the formal education system was underlined in 1960 by the creation of the Instituto Naciónal de Cooperacion Educativa (INCE), an independent system designed to raise the education and training levels of the workers, including the unemployed.

25. Unfortunately, the distribution of firms according to national origin of equity capital did not permit controlling for interindustry effects.

dummies, and (3) using both intercept and slope dummies. Equations of type (1) and (2) gave significant results, indicating that foreign firms do pay higher wages. When both slope and intercept dummies were used, type (3), all dummy variables became nonsignificant, probably as a result of collinearity or insufficient degrees of freedom. As measured by the coefficient of the intercept dummy, the equations indicated that foreign-controlled firms paid wages which are about 17% higher than firms controlled by nationals. The type (2) equation suggests that firms owned by foreigners value education more than firms owned by nationals.

Adjusted occupational differentials

Two types of occupational wage differentials are presented in this section: by occupational category and by specific occupations.

Table 8-6 presents wage estimates and indexes by industry for clerical and production occupations, with clerical wages as the base. This table fails to confirm the hypothesis of systematically higher wages for clerical personnel (white-collar). The fact that in some industries clerical personnel earn less than production personnel, while in other industries the reverse occurs, probably reflects a different demand for labor schedules resulting from unequal production functions and product market conditions. It also suggests inelasticities in the supply of labor, possibly arising from physical barriers to mobility (e.g., transfer costs and deficient communications) and/or institutional effects (such as the influence of labor unions, legislation, and tradition).

Three different regression models were tried to estimate wages for individ-

Table 8-6. Venezuela: Wage indexes and differentials by industry between key clerical and production occupations[a]

Industry	Wage estimates[b]		Wage differentials (Clerical = 100)
	Clerical	Production	
Textiles	5.21	4.47	86
Pharmaceuticals	6.27	7.25	116
Metallurgy	6.26	5.80	93
Vegetable oils	7.84	7.12	91
Household appliances	5.21	7.09	136
Paper	5.21	5.21	100
Cement	5.21	5.69	109
Rubber	5.29	7.12	135
Automobile Assembly	6.13	6.11	100

[a]Wages were estimated on the basis of regression equations.
[b]In Bolivares.

ual occupations. In each model wages were adjusted by a different skill variable.[26] Intercept dummies for occupation were used in every instance. Only responsibility showed a positive coefficient significantly different from zero and this only at the 0.20 level. This might suggest that within a given occupation the variation in wages depends fundamentally on individual skills rather than on formal education. Using this variable for adjusting wage differentials narrows the interoccupational dispersion but does not really alter the unadjusted occupational rank structure presented in a previous section.

Uruguay

The social setting

In 1966 with a gross domestic product per capita of $585 (U.S. dollars), Uruguay had the third highest per capita income in Latin America. Moreover, for years her literacy and life expectancy rates had been among the highest in the region.[27]

In spite of these favorable traits, Uruguay is plagued by economic and social problems. The country suffers a strong and chronic inflation, rising unemployment, an onerous welfare system, and a rigid productive structure. While it took ten years for prices to double during 1945–55, they doubled again during 1955–59, only to redouble during 1959–62 and again during 1962–64.[28]

From 1955 to 1960 gross domestic product at constant market prices (GDP) declined by about 0.2% while industrial gross domestic product (IGDP) grew by about 4.8%. From 1960 to 1965 GDP increased by about 3.9% while IGDP increased by 3.4%. The annual compound rates of growth were about 0.8% and 0.6% respectively. Compared to 1955–57, income per capita in 1964 had fallen by 13%.[29] These figures are suggestive of a stagnant or even a declining economy.

26. Regressions run to adjust for three skill variables in the same equation did not give significant results.

27. Banco Interamericano de Desarrollo, *Progreso Socio-Económico en America Latina, 1967* (Washington, D.C.: Banco Interamericano de Desarrollo, 1968), p. 309.

28. On these and the following points see Comisión de Inversiones y Desarrollo Económico (CIDE), *Plan Nacional de Desarrollo Económico y Social 1965–1974,* vol. 1 (Montevideo, Uruguay: CECEA, 1966), pp. 17, 48–49, 188, 203; George Pendle, *Uruguay* (London: Oxford University Press, 1963), p. 89; Marvin Alisky, *Uruguay a Contemporary Survey* (New York: Praeger, 1969), pp. 86–89.

29. From CIDE, *Plan Nacional de Desarrollo,* p. 178, and figures in Banco Central del Uruguay, *Producto e Ingreso Nacionales* (Montevideo, 1971), pp. 45, 46, and 57. In this last source the industrial sector includes mines and quarries (of little economic importance in Uruguay).

Growth in surveyed industries

Four industries were surveyed for the present study: textiles, pharmaceuticals, metallurgy, and household appliances. During 1955–69, and in the 1960–65, 1964–65 subperiods, data on rates of growth of output for industries that are likely to be representative of the industries surveyed show negative rates for at least one of the periods and subperiods.[30] Furthermore, except for metallurgy, which consistently shows declining rates, the behavior of the other industries varies across periods and subperiods. Under these conditions setting up a hypothesis about probable wage ranks based on industrial growth does not seem worthwhile.

In terms of gross domestic product per worker, as of 1963 pharmaceuticals had the highest average productivity per worker, with textiles, metallurgy, and electric household appliances following successively. It is of interest to determine whether there is a direct correspondence between interindustry productivity levels and relative wage rates by industry.

The sample consisted of six textiles firms, eight pharmaceutical, and four household appliance firms. Data on size of firm are available for every firm except for one in electric products and two in metallurgy. The firms' sizes do not differ considerably among industries—except in pharmaceuticals which seems to have significantly smaller firms. Two firms had fewer than 30 employees, three had 400 or more; almost 64% of the firms had 149 employees or less. The sample contains 348 wage observations, of which 160 correspond to key occupations. Except for operator of industrial machines and engineer, all key occupations have 12 observations or more.

Wage differentials unadjusted by worker skills

INTERINDUSTRY DIFFERENTIALS

Tables 8-7 and 8-8 present average wages and indexes measuring interindustry differentials and rank by occupational categories: table 8-7 based on all occupations in the sample and table 8-8 on key occupations only.[31]

A review of both tables reveals that the only common characteristic in the two orderings is that household appliances pays the lowest wages. In contrast to what happens when all occupations are considered, when only key occupations are taken into account, the interindustry dispersion within production occupations is greater than within clerical occupations.[32]

---

30. Banco Central del Uruguay, *Producto e Ingreso Nationales,* pp. 56–57.

31. Since observations for various key production occupations in pharmaceuticals were nonexistent, this industry is not included in this comparison.

32. A comparison of the results in tables 8-7 and 8-8 with those presented in a work by the

Table 8-7. Uruguay: Interindustry wage differentials by occupational
category, unadjusted by worker skills for all occupations
(Textiles = 100)

Industry	Clerical			Production		
	Wage[a]	Index	Rank	Wage[a]	Index	Rank
Textiles	32.91	100	(2)	29.08	100	(1)
Pharmaceuticals	27.41	83	(3)	26.76	92	(2)
Metallurgy	37.20	113	(1)	25.61	88	(3)
Household appliances	27.15	82	(4)	22.95	79	(4)
Interindustry range		31			21	

[a]Mean wage in Uruguayan pesos.

Table 8-8. Uruguay: Interindustry wage differentials by
occupational category, unadjusted by worker skills
for key occupations (Textiles = 100)

Industry	Clerical			Production		
	Wage[a]	Index	Rank	Wage[a]	Index	Rank
Textiles	24.81	100	(1)	34.23	100	(1)
Pharmaceuticals[b]	22.26	90	(3)	-	-	-
Metallurgy	24.19	97	(2)	33.11	97	(2)
Household appliances	22.19	89	(4)	28.41	83	(3)
Interindustry range		11			17	

[a]Mean wage in Uruguayan pesos.
[b]No figures are shown for production occupations in pharmaceuticals as no observations
are available.

A comparison of the interindustry differentials in table 8-7 with the industrial productivity noted earlier shows that textiles and metallurgy, which have similar productivity levels, also have similar wage levels, and that household appliances, which has the lowest productivity level, also has the lowest wage level. Although pharmaceuticals had the highest productivity per worker, this industry occupied the third rank according to clerical wage rates paid.

Uruguayan Confederation of Workers shows a weak positive correspondence between the sets of findings. This divergence underlines again the importance of controlling for factors such as occupation and industry as well as the wage concept used. See Confederación Uruguaya de Trabajadores, *Realidad Económica Salarial en Uruguay* (Montevideo, 1970), p. 21.

INTERFIRM AND INTRAOCCUPATIONAL WAGE DISPERSION

Computation of coefficients of variation of wages by key occupation, occupational category, and industry show that dispersion in household appliances was considerably smaller than in any of the other industries, and the ordering by wage dispersion was identical to the ordering by wage levels. So the higher the relative wage level in an industry, the higher the intraindustry dispersion tends to be. This could indicate that workers in high wage industries have a greater attachment to their relatively high paying firms.

Within occupations, production occupations showed more dispersion than clerical occupations, suggesting more homogeneity within the latter occupations and / or a more competitive situation within them. The occupations with the greatest dispersion were the highest paid—engineer, cashier, and foreman. This might mean that once an employee attains a high level of renumeration within a firm, nonpecuniary factors such as stability and recognition are valued more than a possible salary increase resulting from a change of job. In any event, high paid employees become less mobile.

Overall, textile and metallurgical firms differ considerably in the way they settle wage demands, while household appliance and pharmaceutical firms settle in a similar manner. Clerical occupations show a greater degree of wage clustering than production occupations.

INTEROCCUPATIONAL WAGE DIFFERENTIALS

Table 8-9 presents wage indexes by key occupational category and industry, using janitor's wages as the base.[33]

As shown in the table, engineers, who are college graduates, earned over five times more than janitors, who are unskilled workers. Lathe operators earn higher wages than typists in metallurgy and household appliances, but less in textiles. Electricians, however, earn less than typists in both textiles and metallurgy but earn more in household appliances. A semiskilled worker, a driver, earns more than a typist in all industries except in pharmaceuticals. As measured by the wage differential between accounting clerks and lathe operators, skilled white-collar employees tend to earn more than their manual labor counterparts. A review of the indexes in table 8-9 shows considerable lack of uniformity across industries in the behavior of the occupational indexes. Across industries and within occupations, the greatest wage fluctuations take place in the high paying occupations of engineer and cashier.

33. As previously, unweighted wage means were used. Sensitivity tests performed by weighting the number of employees in some occupations gave results similar to the ones presented.

Table 8-9. Uruguay: Interoccupational wage differentials by
industry for key occupations (Janitor = 100)

Occupation	Textiles	Pharmaceuticals	Metals	Household appliances	Mean[a]
File clerk	133	120	121	100	118
Typist	150	181	147	121	139
Invoice clerk	163	131	129	121	137
Accounting clerk	198	132	189	191	193
Cashier	262	177	259	211	243
Mean for clerical occupations	181	148	169	149	166
Janitor	100	100	100	100	100
Lathe operator	142	-[b]	182	153	156
Electrician	106	-[b]	144	133	128
Driver	182	160	161	136	159
Engineer	722	-[b]	488	396	531
Foreman	247	173	323	225	265
Mean for production occupations	250	-[b]	233	191	224

[a]Estimated without including pharmaceuticals.
[b]No observations.

Summarizing the main points and implications, wage differentials in Uruguay seem to be narrow when compared to the findings in other developing economies. In other countries at a comparable stage of development skilled and/or semiskilled workers frequently earn twice as much as unskilled workers.[34] The situation in Uruguay is probably the consequence of minimum wage legislation and inflation, two factors which may compress occupational differentials.[35] For example, inflation may stimulate wage legislation providing greater benefits for low income earners. Another factor probably acting in the same direction is the relatively great supply of skilled workers.

34. Gunter, "Changes in Wage Differentials," p. 143; Koji Taira, "Wage Differentials in Developing Countries: A Survey of Findings," *International Labour Review* 93 (June 1966), pp. 281–301. In Uruguay the mean wage of lathe operator, electrician, driver, and foreman is 1.77 times the wage of janitor in textiles, metallurgy, and household appliances when taken as a group. It is lower in textiles and household appliances.

35. See for example, N. N. Franklin, "Minimum Wage Fixing and Economic Development" in *Wage Policy Issues in Economic Development*, ed. A. D. Smith (London: Macmillan 1969; New York: St. Martin's Press, 1969), pp. 338–53; Lloyd G. Reynolds and Peter Gregory, *Wages, Productivity, and Industrialization in Puerto Rico* (Homewood, Ill: Irwin, 1965),

Wage differentials adjusted for worker skills and establishment variables

This subsection discusses the greater ability to explain wage rate variations when establishment and skill variables are considered in the context of regression analysis. As in the case of Venezuela, wages are regressed against skill variables in the first step and then establishment variables are successively introduced. The general linearized model is the same as the one used in the analysis of the Venezuelan differentials, using observations corresponding mainly to key occupations.

When the wages corresponding to key occupations are regressed against the skill variables, about 38% of total wage dispersion is accounted for. The coefficients of the three skill variables—education, experience, and responsibility—are positive, with education and responsibility significant at the 0.10 level, the latter being the most influential variable. If the whole sample is considered—key and non-key occupations—skill variables account for 57% of wage dispersion and all the coefficients are positive and significant at the 0.10 level. As with the key occupations, experience is the least powerful variable and responsibility is the most powerful.

Size of firms and industry dummy variables make no net contribution to the regression containing skill variables. However when skill variables, size of industry, and firm dummy variables are jointly considered, $\bar{R}^2$ rises from 0.38 to 0.40 for a net gain of only 2% after adjusting for degree of freedom.

When occupation dummy variables are added, a considerable increase in $\bar{R}^2$ takes place, from 0.38 to 0.62. While responsibility remains significantly different from zero, education does not, suggesting collinearity between education and the occupation dummy variables. As pointed out previously, this might indicate that education has little effect on wage variations within a given occupation. Although its t ratio rises to very near the critical value at 0.10, experience remains nonsignificantly different from zero. Nevertheless, the results suggest that experience is more important than education in explaining wage rate variation within specific occupations.

In summary, skill and occupational variables jointly explain about 62% of the wage rate dispersion after adjusting for degrees of freedom.

IMPACT ON WAGE DIFFERENTIALS BY INDUSTRY AND OCCUPATIONAL CATEGORY

This subsection focuses on the variation in the effect of workers' skills and size of firm upon wages among industries and occupations. Observations

---

pp. 55; Richard Perlman, "A Note on the Measurement of Real Wage Differentials", *Review of Economics and Statistics* 41 (May 1959), pp. 192–95.

corresponding to all occupations in the sample were used. It was not possible to restrict the experiment to observations corresponding to only key occupations due to the small number of degrees of freedom this entailed.

Skill and/or interindustry effects were able to explain a higher proportion of wage rate variation within clerical occupations than within production occupations. For the former, $\bar{R}^2$ equaled 0.76; for the latter, it was 0.55. In both occupational categories responsibility was the most influential variable and education the least.

Across industries there was more variation in the effect of the skill variables within clerical occupations than within production occupations. Within clerical occupations at least one of the skill coefficients in every industry differed significantly from those in textiles, and in all industries the impact of responsibility differed significantly from that in textiles. As indicated by a lack of differentiation in the constant term, the mean effect of the variables not included in the regression model did not differ significantly across industries. Within production occupations, in only one industry, metallurgy, do skill coefficients differ significantly from textiles.

The direction of the effect of size upon wage rates changed with occupational category. It was predominantly negative for industrial occupations; only for metallurgy was it positive. On the other hand, it was positive for all clerical occupations.

One reason why size might affect industrial wages negatively is that large firms allow greater specialization in the tasks performed.[36] As the tasks become simpler, lower wages tend to be offered; in addition, the larger the firm the greater the nonpecuniary advantages offered—stability and security, for example. Within clerical occupations it is possible that the positive correlation between size and decrease in job complexity is not as strong.

ADJUSTED INTERINDUSTRY DIFFERENTIALS

Table 8-10 presents the interindustry wage structure that results after adjusting wages for worker skills and for the size of firm. The relative position of each industry varies between clerical and production occupations, with the exception of household appliances. Adjustment by skills decreases interindustry dispersion and causes a substantial difference in the industry rank within industrial occupations.

Production wage rates adjusted for worker skills, firm size, and industrial productivity levels were in positive correspondence (i.e., industries which pay relatively high wages are the ones which have the highest productivity per worker).

36. It should be borne in mind that key and non-key occupations were considered jointly.

Table 8-10. Uruguay: Interindustry differentials adjusted for worker
skills and size of firm (Textiles = 100)

Industry	Clerical[a]		Production[b]	
	Wage[c]	Differential	Wage[c]	Differential
Textiles	25.88	100 (3)	25.18	100 (2)
Pharmaceuticals	28.36	110 (2)	25.67	102 (1)
Metallurgy	29.68	115 (1)	22.52	89 (3)
Household appliances	24.91	96 (4)	21.75	86 (4)
Interindustry range		19		16

[a]Education, experience, responsibility, and size valued at 5, 4, 3, and 179 respectively.
[b]Education, experience, responsibility, and size valued at 4, 3, 3, and 179 respectively.
[c]Estimated in Uruguayan pesos.

Table 8-11. Uruguay: Adjusted wage differentials by
occupational category and industry

Industry	Wage estimates[a]		Wage differentials
	Clerical	Production	(Clerical = 100)
Textiles	24.30	25.18	104
Pharmaceuticals	26.77	25.67	96
Metallurgy	26.29	22.52	86
Household appliances	25.13	21.75	87

[a]In Uruguayan pesos.

ADJUSTED OCCUPATIONAL WAGE DIFFERENTIALS

Occupational categories—Differentials between occupational categories
have been measured after adjusting for worker skills and for size of firm.
These adjustments (table 8-11) show that clerical wages were higher than
production wages in three of the four industries. Accepted at face value,
these seemingly lower production wages give some support to the claim that
in Latin America clerical white-collar workers are paid higher wages than
blue-collar employees. In a country whose economy is relatively stagnant,
existing white-collar/blue-collar differentials probably are an example of
differentials reflecting mainly the effects of tradition.

Specific occupations—Neither regressions by occupation, nor regressions
adjusting for the three skill variables and using intercept dummies for occupation, gave significant results. As an alternative, three regressions were
run using intercept dummies for occupation and adjusting, in each case, for
only one skill variable. Even then, of the three skill variables only experience

showed a coefficient significantly different from zero and that only at the 0.20 level. While previous results were consistent with the hypothesis that education and responsibility are more influential in determining the occupations to which a laborer is to be assigned, in respect to wage variation within occupations, experience becomes the most influential variable. An application could be that if an individual decides not to move to another occupation, a year of experience on the average would raise his wages more than a year of additional education would.

If the interoccupational differentials are adjusted by experience, relative to the unadjusted differentials (table 8-9), the interoccupational wage dispersion is reduced and electricians and file clerks do not emerge with wages differing significantly from those of janitors. Otherwise, adjusting for experience does not alter the occupational ranks.

Policy implications

Based on the foregoing findings this section sets forth a comparative review of some of the characteristics of the Venezuelan and Uruguayan labor markets and offers general policy implications.

A comparison of the dispersion of interoccupational and interindustry wages in Venezuela with those in Uruguay indicates that the results are consistent with the view that wage differentials in less developed countries tend to be wider in growing economies. The difference in wage dispersion between the two countries can be explained by the positive rate of industrial growth in Venezuela and a rising demand for skilled workers that pushed skilled wages high. In Uruguay, in contrast, economic stagnation coupled with the likely wage compressing effects of inflation and minimum wage legislation resulted in comparatively narrow differentials.

Interfirm differentials are, however, narrower in Venezuela. This could be interpreted as indicative of more defined industry wage contours brought about by greater intraindustry labor mobility. In turn, the greater mobility may be the consequence of—among other factors—the relative unimportance of seniority as a wage raising element. In the previous section it was shown that, with respect to intraoccupation wage dispersion, in Uruguay experience was the most influential variable. As experience and seniority can be presumed to be in strong direct correspondence, it would seem that in Uruguay seniority is an important wage determining factor. As seniority acts in the direction of reducing mobility, a segmentation of the labor market at the firm level tends to ensue.

In contrast to the findings in developed countries, unskilled wages do not seem to be more dispersed than skilled wages. While in Venezuela no clear pattern emerged, in Uruguay the wage dispersion of highly paid employees was greater. It was reasoned employees become less mobile in Uruguay when attaining high wage positions.

The overall impact of education seems stronger in Venezuela than in Uruguay, possibly because of the generally lower educational level of the Venezuelan labor force. Another interesting fact is that while in Venezuela responsibility was the single most influential variable in explaining wage variation within occupations, in Uruguay experience was the most influential. This finding is consistent with the hypothesis that Venezuelan entrepreneurs are more willing than their Uruguayan counterparts to reward ability and accomplishment. In contrast, Uruguay seems to place a higher premium on seniority.

The wage structures in both countries indicate that to an extent the labor markets behave competitively. This is supported by the higher wages paid in occupations requiring greater skills and by the fact that skills explain a substantial proportion of wage variation. Since they help to direct labor skills into positions of higher productivity (and wages), these conditions are necessary for efficient performance of the labor markets.

The incentives for attaining higher levels of skill are likely to be stronger in Venezuela where interoccupational differentials are wider. The relatively narrow differentials in Uruguay and the low wages paid in occupations requiring relatively high training—electricians for example—suggest that in this country the wage structure might discourage worker interest in greater skills.

In spite of the characteristics consistent with market competitiveness, various market signals are suggestive of imperfections and inefficiency. As shown in previous sections, considerable dispersion exists in the wage rates for workers having similar skills and in the same occupation. If the differentials were of a short-run nature they would perform an important long-run allocative role. Yet one is led to believe otherwise, considering that in various countries other researchers have found that similar differentials tend to persist and that in the two countries studied here strong elements of imperfections, like pressure groups and inadequate information systems, play an important market role.

An inadequate information system is an important cause of the narrow dispersion of job inefficiency. Not only does it mean that workers are unaware of positions in which their productivities (and wages) are higher, it also means that firms must make employment decisions without adequate information. Can the skills they need be found in the market? Is it less costly to hire these skills or to develop them through training? The answers depend on the relative contract costs and availability of workers already processing the needed skills versus those of training labor.[37] In summary, by diminishing risk and uncertainty, improving the information system of the labor market would promote a more efficient allocation of labor. In view of the indications of strong market imperfections, it would seem that this should be a high priority objective in Venezuela and in Uruguay, if the 1966 conditions found here still hold.

The information mechanism can be improved by setting up accessible offices providing full information on job vacancies and available workers. These centers could also provide job counseling, especially to young workers. To make the centers functional, firms and workers should be encouraged to register and to provide all pertinent information. Note should be taken of the factors that have led to low use of employment exchanges in Venezuela. The extent to which it is worth providing these services is best decided by cost benefit analysis which weighs the cost of providing additional information against the benefits derived from it.[38] Although not enough is known on this issue, information may be a commodity with decreasing costs which calls for public production.[39]

Consideration should be given to other ways of providing for a more competitive performance of the labor markets, such as improving the transportation system, reducing commuting costs and increasing worker mobility, and supervising collective bargaining procedures, preventing either labor unions or employer associations from gaining a position of predominance.

The width of wage differentials in Venezuela suggests that vocational training should be encouraged. This could be achieved either through vocational schools or through training programs provided by the firms. Since to some extent the skills developed through these programs are nonspecific to a single firm or industry and could be used in various sectors, consideration should be given to providing public subsidies for these training efforts.

It has been shown that both in Venezuela and in Uruguay market forces in 1966 seemed to operate more effectively in clerical occupations. Moreover, in Venezuela wage differentials for novice workers are wider, suggesting that for these workers market forces operate less efficiently.[40] These findings

37. Lester Thurow, *Investment in Human Capital*, Wadsworth Series in Labor Economics and Industrial Relations (Belmont, Calif.: Wadsworth, 1970), pp. 30–32, 69–102; George J. Stigler, "Information in the Labor Market," *Journal of Political Economy*, supplement (October 1962), pp. 94–105.

38. Stigler, "Information in the Labor Market."

39. Thurow, *Investment in Human Capital*, p. 31.

40. This comment is based on a comparison of a minimum wage structure with maximum wage differentials. Space constraints prevented the presentation and discussion of the comparison in this chapter.

lead to the conclusion that efforts to improve the operation of the labor market might place major emphasis on the market for production workers and, at least in Venezuela, also for beginners. From a different perspective, wage policy should attempt to correct wage differentials detrimental to growth. For example, in order that skilled/nonskilled differentials be adequate to encourage the acquisition of skills and the use of training centers, efforts may be made to obtain labor union support in preventing unskilled wages from rising as fast as skilled wages. Although this policy might increase short-run inequality in the distribution of income, on the other hand it could help to promote the employment of unskilled labor.[41]

Since wages are an important component of household income, wage inequality is a major determinant of income inequality. Accordingly, the wage structures described in this study can be expected to have counterparts in income distributions, i.e., large skill-wage differentials are likely to be accompanied by considerable inequalities in the distribution of household income. This proportion suggests greater income inequality in Venezuela than in Uruguay among manufacturing workers, which is consistent with income equalizing legislation likely to be more extensive in Uruguay than in Venezuela and the findings of Kuznets, Weisskoff, and Adelman and Morris, that in less developed countries growth leads to greater income inequality.[42]

The positive association between skills and wages suggests that policies aimed at increasing skill levels by providing equal access to education, training, and general ability-developing facilities are likely to have income equalizing effects, and that these effects would probably be stronger in Venezuela. Efforts to increase the productivity of workers should take into consideration that in these models responsibility was important in explaining wage variation. Thus, factors affecting worker alertness and motivation deserve careful investigation.

Research is needed on the wage structures existing in the public sector of developing countries, as well as on the interaction between the public and the private wage structures. It seems that frequently wages in government are not in correspondence with grades of ability and, in general, the public wage

41. Although unsuccessful, an effort in this direction has been made in Jamaica. See the comments of G. C. Bonnick in "A Summary of the Discussions" in *Wage Policy Issues,* ed. A. D. Smith, p. 137.

42. Simon Kuznets, "Quantitative Aspects of the Economic Growth of Nations: VIII. Distribution of Income by Size," *Economic Development and Cultural Change* 2 (January 1963), pp. 1–79; Richard Weisskoff, "Income Distribution and Economic Growth in Puerto Rico, Argentina, and Mexico," *Review of Income and Wealth* 4 (December 1970), pp. 303–31; Irma Adelman and Cynthia Taft Morris, "An Anatomy of Income Distribution Patterns in Developing Nations," *Development Digest* 9, no. 4. (October 1971), pp. 24–37.

structure seems chaotic and irrational.[43] In countries like Uruguay where in terms of direct employment generated the government is an important employer, the wage structure in the private sector may be considerably influenced by the wage structure in the public sector.[44] Accordingly, setting governmental pay scales on the basis of ability and merit would seem a good initial step toward correcting the overall wage structure.

Minimum wage legislation might be a useful tool in attaining a desired change in the wage structure. As shifts in minimum wage have an impact upon the overall structure, it could be used to erase wage differentials which do not reflect differences in skills or working conditions. This is another area of research which deserves careful attention.

To conclude, it should be exphasized that further analysis is needed on the objectives of wage policy. As indicated, wage policy is often used as a redistributive mechanism to attain social objectives. Perhaps it is preferable to reach these through fiscal policies while using relative wages to promote an efficient allocation of labor. In turn, wages could be influenced indirectly by affecting supply and demand schedules for labor, for example, through manpower policies.[45]

43. Berg, "Wage Structures," pp. 318–33; and the comment by H. A. Turner in "A Summary of the Discussions" in *Wage Policy Issues,* ed. Smith, p. 107.

44. N. N. Franklin, "Minimum Wage Fixing and Economic Development" in *Wage Policy Issues,* p. 341.

45. Lloyd G. Reynolds, "Objectives of Wage Policy in Developing Countries," pp. 217–34, and the observations of Clark Kerr, "A Summary of the Discussions," p. 156, in *Wage Policy Issues.*

Chapter 9. Conclusions and implications

This chapter summarizes the most important findings derived in the various parts of this book, discusses their interrelations, and explores their policy implications.

Background

In discussing differentials in wages in the LAFTA region, an aspect of the problem of total income differences is being touched upon. Differences in total income tend to reflect inequalities in the income received from labor because labor income usually constitutes well over half of total income. Thus, labor income differentials can provide an indication of total income differences.

Wage differentials have diverse origins. They can arise from differences in the country or region of residence, in skills, and in industry and firm of employment.[1] Behind these factors lie the real causes of variation in labor income. They include short-run disequilibrium situations, unattractiveness or disutility of the job to the worker, labor productivity, training and moving costs and other labor supply conditions, and imperfections in the labor and product markets.

Some of these causes are impervious to labor policy—short-run disequilibria, for example, and the compensating wage differentials reflecting how workers perceive the relative disutilities of performing certain tasks. It would be practically impossible to eliminate these sources of wage differentials or labor income inequality. Others are more tractable, but may require a judgment of their importance as sources of income inequality, on the one hand, and as signalling devices for market adjustments, on the other. This is so when wage differentials mainly arising from labor productivity, for instance, may act as the mechanisms through which the labor supply structure adjusts to the corresponding structure of labor demand. If adjustments take place in this fashion, the differences found in labor incomes may at least be partly justified. However, some of these productivity differences may be so ingrained that they will never tend to correct themselves, in which case the policy maker may be justified in trying to ameliorate the resulting wage differentials to reduce inequality.

---

1. These can be broken down further, for example, in terms of firm (size, origin of capital, etc.) or skill (education, sex, etc.).

The case is quite different when market imperfections are considered. Here there is no contribution of wage differences to better functioning market mechanisms by signalling scarcities in certain skills, industries, or countries. Rather, the differentials may strictly contribute to income inequality, involving quasi-rents to particular kinds of labor.[2] Thus, it is obvious that policies to eliminate market imperfections should be welcome not only to eliminate allocative inefficiencies but also to mitigate income inequality.

In this study wage differentials according to country (region), skills, industry, and firm were measured. It is important to speculate on the extent to which these differentials indicate the relative importance of the underlying causes mentioned above. Particularly useful would be to get an impression of the relative importance of those causes that can be affected by policy, especially the crucial ones: transfer and training costs on the one hand and market imperfections on the other.[3] Yet, before proceeding with this attempt, the size and nature of the various wage differences estimated in this study should be reviewed together with its other major findings, and revised in the light of more recent wage data.

Major findings of the study

Intracountry differentials

Previous chapters have documented that the interskill differentials appear to be very wide within the region. In terms of net wages or take-home pay for the various occupations and industries covered in the study, the wages of a worker with seven or eight years of education and about two years experience, are generally twice those of a worker with three or four years of formal training and about two months experience (see chapter 4). As would be expected, the greater the dispersion in the skills being compared, the wider the divergence in wages.

From the various country chapters it was also seen that the ratio of starting or minimum wages for skilled employees to those of unskilled employees (usually defined as a janitor) was a little over two. To obtain a more realistic impression of actual differences, it should be noted that in Venezuela the same skilled to unskilled wage ratio is nearly doubled once the maximum wages of the skilled categories are considered.

2. As suggested in chapter 2, if it were not for market imperfections, especially in the markets for labor services, wage differentials could be explained just in terms of training and transfer costs and job unattractiveness, except for those resulting from short-run disequilibria.

3. These are the two main elements of wage differentials once short run and job disutility conditions are excluded. Labor productivity and other labor supply conditions basically influence the differentials because of or through market imperfections and transfer and training costs.

The ratio is higher for particular positions and countries. For example, if the engineering trainee is considered as the skilled position in the comparison, the skilled/unskilled ratio would be close to six in Venezuela. The same ratio would be about four if cashier is considered as the skilled occupation, as in the case of Colombia. The former ratio would be close to the ratio of average earnings of the highest paid professional position to minimum wage earnings in the United States, which indicates that skill differentials are greater in Latin America. The evidence suggests that in general, other conditions equal, a high premium is paid for formal education and training.

Intercountry differentials

Wage differentials across countries appear to be very wide. Taking the country with lowest wages as a base, the country with the highest wages was usually three times above it. Curiously, these wage differences appear to be of a similar order of magnitude as the interskill differentials within each country. If the wage differentials are considered in real rather than money terms, the relative intercountry range shrinks somewhat, to less than 2.5.

For intercountry differentials it is important to make the comparisons in real terms because of the different purchasing power of the various Latin American currencies. In fact, as can be surmised from the narrowing of the intercountry differentials, countries with higher wages usually have a higher cost of living, and vice versa.

For several purposes it is useful to consider to what extent intercountry comparisons in terms of labor costs differ from those based on wages. After using the same exchange rates to convert wages and labor costs into a common currency, it is evident that the results are quite different, with rankings and wage relatives being affected. In particular, there is less dispersion in terms of labor costs, which include fringe benefits and social provision concepts that are not part of take-home pay. This principally affects the Southern Cone countries, which appear to have higher fringe benefits and social provisions, and suggests that these elements may be considered substitutes for straight wages.

Interindustry differentials

Within the LAFTA countries, interindustry differentials were found to be much smaller than those due to differences in skills, and are relatively unimportant contributors to labor income differentials.[4] The relative ranges of

4. In fact, because the industries with high and low wages in the various LAFTA countries are not always the same industries, the large internal differences in industry wages cancel each other out, and the LAFTA wage average for each industry is practically the same for the textile and pharmaceutical industries, and just a bit higher for metallurgy. This suggests that there is no clear pattern of high and low paying industries in the area.

interindustry differentials tend to fluctuate between 20% and 60% (see chapters 4, 7, and 8).

Another major type of wage differentials, those found *across firms,* were found to be relatively small in the results reported in chapter 4. However, these refer only to a certain range of variation in size of firm (100 to 1,000 employees approximately), and to the modern part of the manufacturing sector. As suggested in chapter 8, interfirm differentials might have been larger if other firm characteristics, rather than size of firm, had been used (origin of the firm's capital, technological advancement, etc.), if some sort of overall or composite index of firm attributes had been tried, or if size had been permitted to vary more. In general it would appear that interfirm differentials were somewhat higher than interindustry differentials, but still much lower than interskill wage differences.[5] In itself, the above suggests that in order to improve his wage position, a person would do better if he were able to move across occupations rather than across firms and industries. This applies even if one excludes such extreme positions as engineer and janitor. Naturally, this once again points to the importance of education or on the job training and underlines the need to study in greater depth the determinants of the internal wage structure (e.g. within firms).

Effects of the variables considered on wages

Overall, two thirds or more of the variation in real wages is explained by skill and establishment variables plus the intercountry dummies. Not only is it a large part of the total variation, but its relative constancy is surprising. Most of the explanation can be attributed to the skill variables (qualitative requirements) and the country dummies, as the establishment variable (size of firm) adds only marginally to the explanation. In similar attempts at an explanation of wage variation, the degrees of explanation attained have been smaller. Giora Hanoch, for example, has suggested that between personal (skill) and establishment variables 45%–50% of the total variation can usually be explained.[6]

Country slope coefficients, picking up the interaction between the qualitative requirements and the country variables, have an important effect on the explanation of wage differentials. These variables, when significant, indicate that the returns to each skill factor (education, experience, responsibility) vary across countries. Hence, since the returns or implicit prices for these factors differ in the various countries, the wage differentials are not uniform

5. Only in the case of Colombia were intracountry regional differentials calculated. These differentials were found to be over twice the size of the wage differences among industries, even though they referred only to the largest cities in Colombia.
6. Giora Hanoch, "Personal Earnings and Investment in Schooling" (Ph.D. diss., University of Chicago, 1965).

throughout their range, and the comparisons must cover combinations of the values of the skill variables, if they are to reflect reality.

Another important result is that intercountry wage differentials change substantially after wages are adjusted by the various skill factors represented in job content. This stems from the interplay of wages with the qualitative factors, and points out the importance of isolating or netting out the effects of these factors before measuring real wage differences among countries.

In particular, wage dispersion is generally lessened after adjustment for the skill factors. This suggests that usually high wages are connected with high skill requirements, and low wages with low skill requirements, within the LAFTA area. As a result, the intercountry wage spread is narrowed after adjustment for labor skills. However, the extent to which the differences in labor incomes are narrowed varies by industry, especially in terms of which countries become higher or lower after adjustment.

After real wages have been adjusted for the skill factors and computed for each industry and country, no pattern of skill differentials emerges. The ratios of high to low wages vary by country and within them, according to the industry examined, and most hover around a value of two.

With respect to the real wage comparisons and size of firm, including the establishment variable improves explanation, but not by much. This could be interpreted as indicating a positive association between size and overall skill level.

Wage differentials for the same occupation

When the intercountry wage differentials were estimated originally, the occupational characteristics of the workers were permitted to vary under the hypothesis that it would not matter much after the influence of other skill variables (education, etc.) had been removed. Later on this factor was introduced. It was found that intercountry wage differentials before and after controlling for occupation were largely coincidental in terms of rankings and wage relatives, giving support to this hypothesis. More dispersion was noted after occupation was controlled, probably due to the fact that the number of observations is reduced when only wages for the same occupation are considered across countries.

The occupational indices were consistent for the various occupations considered, understandably bearing a greater resemblance when clerical positions were considered on the one hand, and production positions on the other. The rankings, and the pattern of high, middle, and low countries, were particularly similar among the former.

An interesting conclusion from contrasting the intercountry wage differentials for clerical and production occupations within LAFTA is that the ratios of the wages of clerical workers to those of production workers were low in Argentina and Uruguay, compared with the rest of the LAFTA countries. The contrary was true for Venezuela and Chile.

Results at the country level

From the analysis of the structure of wages in Colombia, Mexico, Venezuela, and Uruguay, useful generalizations can be derived at a more detailed level. One is that labor skill or job content differences among firms and industries (at least in the modern manufacturing sector) within each country appear to be significant, but not great, especially for the same occupation.[7] This follows from the fact that the various intracountry wage differentials do not change radically after adjustment for job content.

Of the qualitative variables used for determining job content—education, responsibility, and experience—the first two seem to be the more influential in the determination of wages, which is not surprising for education. The more interesting result relates to responsibility, which may highlight the importance of this variable in determining the intrinsic productivity of labor.

The weak relationship between experience and wages, especially for production workers, is also food for thought.[8] This may result from the following factors:

1. Rapid expansion of the modern manfacturing sector, needing to delve into the relatively young and inexperienced segment of the labor force.

2.Preference for on the job training by the firms in question.

3. Irrelevance of previous experience to the tasks to be performed in modern manufacturing, of relatively recent origin in most of the countries examined.

4. Lack of or weak unionization. It is to be remembered that unionization usually involves the establishment of seniority rules having a beneficial effect on experienced workers.

In general, the positive relationship between qualitative requirements and wages found in the various countries suggests that the labor markets do tend to balance supply and demand for different skills. Higher skills are being more highly compensated, and therefore wages are acting as an efficient signaling device. Other evidence, such as significant interindustry and interfirm differentials for homogeneously defined positions, suggests inefficien-

7. This stands in contrast with the much larger differences that were found among countries, and explains why the occupational variable did not appear to matter much in intercountry wage differences while in some cases being important to the analysis of intracountry wage differences.

8. Uruguay is somewhat of an exception here, probably due to the influence of the seniority system in that country.

cies in labor market performance and that market imperfections are an important determinant in the misallocation of labor encountered in Latin American countries.

The variation of the skilled/unskilled wage ratios and of the interfirm differences among the countries appears to be related to the growth of these economies in the second part of the 60s. Mexico had the wider wage structure, followed by Colombia and then Venezuela. Uruguay showed narrower interskill and interfirm differentials. This jibes with the hypothesis of higher demand pressures being exerted by an expanding economy, which would originate, given the same conditions of labor supply elasticity, higher wage premiums for scarce skills and new jobs in expanding firms and industries.

Updating some of the results

The labor structures summarized here refer to the end of 1966, and it would be useful to consider wage levels for more recent dates. However, because the wage structure changes slowly, it can be expected that the conclusions referring to it would still be valid at these later dates.

The more recent results show important changes in wage levels since the end of 1966. The overall labor cost indices for a sample of modern manufacturing sectors (table 9-1) show that Mexico, Venezuela, and Brazil had the highest labor costs at the end of 1970, with Mexico in particular being far above the LAFTA average. These results are not surprising, except for Brazil, where money wages were comparatively low at the end of 1966. The fast industrial growth experienced by Brazil appears to have generated increasing tightness in the labor markets in that country, giving rise to sharp increases in wages and fringe benefits. Another contributing factor, given that official exchange rates are used for conversion purposes in this comparison, is a relative appreciation of the Brazilian cruzeiro with respect to the other LAFTA currencies.

If the low end of the scale is considered, the position of Ecuador did not vary much since the end of 1966. The same could be said of Bolivia, which seemed to have significantly higher labor costs than Ecuador at the end of 1970. The relatively low standing of Peru, between the previous two countries, requires some explanation. A large devaluation of the Peruvian currency, the sol, might be part of it. A curbing of the unions and increasing government control of wages and fringe benefits might also help to explain what seems to have been a much slower increase of labor costs in the modern manufacturing sector in Peru.[9]

9. Other noticeable intertemporal changes are the relative decrease in Colombian labor costs and the relative increase of those in Uruguay.

Table 9-1. Overall index of labor costs for a sample of
industries in the LAFTA countries, November 1970[a]
(LAFTA average = 100)

Country	Index	Rank
Argentina	110	(4)
Bolivia	66	(9)
Brazil	136	(3)
Chile	95	(5)
Colombia	80	(7)
Ecuador	40	(11)
Mexico	214	(1)
Paraguay	71	(8)
Peru	44	(10)
Uruguay	93	(6)
Venezuela	151	(2)

[a]This index is the result of combining and aggregating the individual industry indexes for textiles, pharmaceutical, and metallurgy. Imputations were made for the missing industries in Mexico and Bolivia.

As noted earlier, when comparing income or wages across countries it is important to do so in real terms, since purchasing power varies substantially among nations. Thus, for a similar wage, differing prices for the wage goods may bring about significant differences in levels of living. To accomplish such real wage comparisons the labor income data have to be converted into a common currency unit by means of purchasing power parity rates.[10]

An index of real wages for LAFTA countries in November 1970 is presented in table 9-2, with real wages defined on a net take-home pay basis. It is a combined relative wage level for the same sample of modern manufacturing sectors just discussed. The exchange rate, which could cause changes in the country standings over time, is completely isolated in this case, having no influence over the results.

The same countries that have the highest labor costs also appear to have the highest real wages. The difference between Mexico, Venezuela, and Brazil and the rest of the countries narrows, which would appear to suggest that wages and wage good prices move in the same direction, and partially counterbalance each other.

10. The purchasing power parity rates for the end of 1970 were derived in another ECIEL study. Jorge Salazar-Carrillo, *Price, Purchasing Power, and Real Product Comparisons in Latin America* (Washington, D.C.: OAS/ECIEL, 1978).

Table 9-2. Overall index of real wages for sample
industries in the LAFTA countries, November 1970[a]
(LAFTA average = 100)

Country	Index	Rank
Argentina	85	(8)
Bolivia	68	(10)
Brazil	120	(3)
Chile	110	(5)
Colombia	71	(9)
Ecuador	68	(11)
Mexico	154	(1)
Paraguay	91	(6)
Peru	111	(4)
Uruguay	87	(7)
Venezuela	140	(2)

[a]This index is the result of combining and aggreagating the individual industry indexes for textiles, pharmaceuticals, and metallurgy. Imputations were made for the missing industries in Mexico
and Bolivia.

As with the labor costs index, Ecuador and Bolivia had the lowest wage
levels in LAFTA at the end of 1970, but Colombia had supplanted Peru as the
third low wage country. In fact the position of Peru was much higher in
terms of real wages, suggesting a relatively low cost of living there, as well
as lower social security deductions.

The main intertemporal variations appear again to affect Brazil, and to a
lesser extent Colombia and Argentina. It would appear that real wages have
grown noticeably in the first country, while dropping significantly in the
latter two.

Data for 1973, the most recent information available on manufacturing
wages at the end of 1976, would suggest that from 1970 to 1973 the intercountry wage and labor cost indices experienced little change. These rates of
change of wages adjusted for inflation appear in table 9-3. The outstanding
features are an apparent narrowing of the differentials between Mexico, Venezuela, and Brazil due to a continuation of the high growth rate of manufacturing wages in the latter and a relatively low one in Venezuela and especially Mexico. Other traits worth mentioning are the apparent fall in the
relative wage level of Colombia and its rise in Bolivia and Peru.[11]

11. Refer to International Labor Office, *Yearbook of Labor Statistics 1975* (Geneva: ILO
1975).

Table 9-3. Average annual rates of change in
manufacturing wages in the LAFTA countries, 1970–73
(Adjusted for inflation)

Country	Percent
Argentina	1.0
Bolivia	9.3
Brazil[a]	9.8
Chile	−2.5
Colombia	−10.0
Ecuador	4.4
Mexico	0.4
Paraguay	n.a.
Peru	9.0
Uruguay	−1.5
Venezuela	2.0

SOURCE: International Labor Office, *Yearbook of Labor Statistics
1975* (Geneva: I.L.O., 1975).
[a] Corresponding to 1970–72.
n.a. = Not available.

Major policy implications

This study has shown the existence of substantial wage differences within
and between Latin American countries, with differences in skills accounting
for a major part of the dispersion of wages in the LAFTA region. Differences
betwen skilled and unskilled worker wages in Latin America are larger than
those for highly industrialized countries, such as the United States.

Having clearly established the relative importance of the various wage
differentials it is not possible to make inferences about their basic underlying
causes. It seems that intercountry wage differentials do not just reflect the
transfer costs involved. Rather, as their size makes evident, they result basically from barriers to labor mobility and other market imperfections, such as
lack of information.[12]

It should be recognized, however, that although intercountry differences
are rather large at the extremes of the wage rankings presented in chapter 4,
they are much narrower for certain subsets of countries. Although in this
case the size of the differences would seem to approximate compensating

12. Part of these wage differentials probably are of a compensating kind anyway. A higher
real wage in a neighboring country may not attract labor from a particular country because of
job disutilities. In other words, workers normally prefer to work in their own country rather
than to accept a higher real wage in another one, as long as the difference is not too large.

differentials plus transfer costs, this probably is not a consequence of mobility or other labor market forces, but rather a reflection of similar production, labor supply, and market conditions in these subsets of countries.

The wide labor income differentials due to varying skills appear to reflect a combination of high training costs and market imperfections. It is impossible to say to what extent each contributes to the wide interskill differentials found. Market imperfections, including monopoly elements, may give rise to important quasi-rents for certain skills. Yet, interskill wage differences would seem to respond mostly to variations in the training costs required to acquire the skills in question.

Intercountry inequalities and integration policies

To the extent that these differences still exist in the present, as is very likely, income distribution policy within LAFTA should take into consideration some of the points just made. In particular, the very large differences existing among LAFTA countries have relevance for integration policies in the area, which have to take into consideration the distribution of income not only within, but also among the countries involved.

Integration policies can consider this problem in two ways. One would involve direct attempts to redistribute income among the countries. A possibility suggested by this study would be to facilitate the movement of labor among countries as a form of alleviating the large labor income differences generally found. In this manner, it could be expected that real take-home pay would increase faster in low wage countries like Bolivia and Ecuador, and slower in high wage countries like Venezuela, Mexico, and Brazil.

The second way of facing the intercountry income distribution issue is an indirect approach, such as providing for slower convergence to a common external tariff, permitting higher tariffs for low income countries, instituting a more lenient foreign investment code for these nations, etc.

An important advantage of a direct income distribution policy through labor mobility is that apart from its redistributive effects, it also provides for improved economic efficiency for the region as a whole through a better allocation of human resources. Yet it would probably be more difficult to implement this policy measure than others having a comparable effect in terms of country redistribution of the net benefits of integration. This is because, with practically no exceptions, there is an employment problem in the LAFTA countries consisting of substantial rates of open unemployment and even higher rates of underemployment. Thus the countries generally do not wish to liberalize their immigration and labor legislations, through which the inflow of labor is usually controlled.

From the real wage levels calculated after adjusting for skills and other variables, some inferences can be made about possible labor migration among the Latin American countries. The main one is that labor should flow from Bolivia, Ecuador, and Colombia to Venezuela and Brazil, in South America, at least under the conditions existing in 1973. This was mostly borne out by the known movement in the area. Mexico's attractiveness in terms of real wages is compensated by the distance from the other countries, which neutralizes to a large extent its pulling force. If labor movement is liberalized in Latin America, the flow of workers from Bolivia, Ecuador, and Colombia to other countries in the southern or northern part of the hemisphere would probably be intensified, with more persons perhaps reaching Venezuela, Brazil, and Mexico.

It should be pointed out that the real wage indices presented in table 9-2 are composites of various occupations, industries, and job contents. If the wage structures are considered in greater detail as was done in chapter 4, it becomes evident that the real wage differentials among countries vary according to the kind of labor being considered. Thus, the labor movements across the LAFTA borders would not necessarily be unidirectional. This is also attested to by the migration flows that have actually been taking place in Latin America, with higher skills being interchanged with lower skills between two countries, as in the workers' exchange between Argentina and Paraguay.

It is well known that trade can be a substitute for factor movements, although its wage equalization properties are still debated. Thus, policies promoting an increase in intra–Latin American trade may be considered a feasible alternative given the barriers to labor mobility that these countries have erected. In this context it should be noticed that the intercountry comparisons show that labor costs are usually directly related to income per capita, within LAFTA. The poorest countries (which also happen to be the smallest in terms of population) have a labor cost advantage. As has been pointed out in chapter 5, this would suggest that, other things equal, they could potentially have better export prospects especially in labor intensive goods.[13]

However, Colombia does not have high labor costs either, is more developed, and would appear to have more sophisticated marketing know-how, while having a larger market and perhaps lower capital costs. Thus, at the end of 1973 the prospects for manufacturing exports from Colombia seemed

13. It was made clear in that chapter that a labor cost advantage only indicated a potential trade advantage, as labor and total costs per unit of output are influenced by other factors apart from labor costs, like capital labor ratios and capital costs. However, it is felt that labor costs are one of the important determinants of trade advantages because they constitute the principal component of total costs, and have been adjusted by various factors related to productivity (like labor quality) in the comparisons presented in this study.

even better than those of Ecuador, Bolivia, and Paraguay. In the case of Brazil the sharp rise experienced in its labor costs from the end of 1966 may have compensated to a great extent the other favorable factors that determined its apparent trade advantage in 1966.

It should be noted that the other labor cost advantage situations appeared to be stable during the 1966–73 period. However, as the detailed examination undertaken in chapter 5 indicates, the labor cost advantages are not uniform, implying that there is room for specialization within the LAFTA area in manufacturing trade.

In order to alleviate income differences within integration movements, and in particular labor income differences, policies to foster labor mobility, or to complement it through increasing trade liberalization, are either considered difficult to implement or are judged to have weak effects. Yet the labor cost differences presented throughout the book suggest that the net benefits to be reaped from facilitating the direct or indirect (through trade) integration of the labor markets in the area would be large. On the other hand, whether legally or not, labor migration has augmented substantially in Latin America in the last decade and will be increasingly difficult to control in the years to come. The bringing down of barriers to labor mobility on a gradual basis may end up providing a posteriori approval of facts.

In summary, in order to diminish intercountry labor income differences and redistribute the net benefits of integration more justly, serious consideration should be given to bringing down the obstacles to labor mobility in the region, preferably in a direct fashion but also through the indirect means of increased trade. Not only would this contribute effectively to reducing income inequality in the region, but the interconnection of the labor markets in the area would improve their performance as allocators of different kinds of labor, both on a country and on a regional basis. Then, in contrast with other policies which redistribute the net benefits of integration, the economic improvement is provided directly to persons in need, avoiding the dangers of dilution presented by intergovernmental transfers and the apportionment of production incentives. Finally, sizable migration promotes, as no other intercountry exchange does, the fuller integration of the area, which is the ultimate goal of the various regional schemes existing in Latin America.

Given that a gradualistic policy is recommended, and that the flows are not expected to be unidirectional, it would seem that the dangers of upheaval in the labor markets of certain Latin American countries, which are commonly foreseen, are somewhat exaggerated. Immigrant labor, it should be kept in mind, usually does not compete frontally with domestic labor, being drawn to jobs where scarcities have developed. Even when competition arises, it can be argued that it has a salutary effect on investment, production, and trade, by keeping down labor costs.

National policies to reduce skill differentials

The wide interskill differentials, which represent the other major source of labor income inequality in the LAFTA area, have special implications for educational and training policies, as they mostly would seem to result from differences in training costs. However, because other factors are involved, some of which are very difficult to influence (family status, intelligence, motivation, etc.), in addition to training policies more general income distribution measures, through incomes and fiscal policies, would seem to be needed.

At the same time, there are certain limitations in which labor income differentials should be reduced. Such differences have an allocative function also, as long as they do not reflect market imperfections. The wage differentials due to the latter should be minimized, of course, but those not related to some sort of monopoly power (or those seen as very ingrained and unjust) should be handled with care unless the government is prepared to use manpower policy as a replacement for market signaling.

A good illustration of the interplay of these strands is provided by the fact, uncovered in the study, that clerical workers generally earn more than production workers. The training costs of the former are higher than those of the latter, being the main cause of the wage differential. The differential is probably higher than the costs involved so as to signal that there is a net benefit to acquiring the clerical skills. If the government meddles with this differential, it may end up thwarting the operation of the labor markets and creating an undersupply or oversupply of clerical workers, having adverse consequences for the operation of the economic system. As a country develops and the training of its labor force increases, the supply and demand conditions for clerical and production workers compress this wage differential, after some time.

Unfortunately, in Latin America the labor markets do not appear to work all that smoothly, being more imperfect than those in the United States and other advanced countries, even though the signaling mechanisms seem to be in operation. This conclusion has been inferred mainly from the wide differentials found in the various countries examined in the study.[14]

These imperfections require the use of labor policies to pare down intra-

14. The reader should be reminded that some of these were net differentials, that is with the wages adjusted to reflect a common set of qualitative and other variables.

country differentials, so that they would better reflect market forces and constitute proper incentives. These would motivate the potential or actual members of the labor force to invest in their own education and training in order to acquire scarce skills. Governments would support these decisions through appropriate educational and training policies.

Generally, too much emphasis has been placed in Latin America on educational policies as a form of improving the intrinsic productivity of the labor force. In fact, even informal education has been somewhat slighted until recently. The lessons provided by the study suggest that new avenues toward the improvement of the capacity and skills of the workers should be explored. The fact that industrial experience does not appear to be appreciated by employers, and the preference that seems to be given to on-the-job training, suggests that policies should be adopted that support the employers' training schemes and enrich the working experience of the industrial labor force. Then, the impact that responsibility seems to have on the intrinsic productivity of labor stresses the importance that should be given to elements such as initiative, alertness, motivation, and responsibility. It is true that some of these factors are difficult to change except at an early age. However, others may be influenced by training programs, and this merits further research, especially as they remain untouched by present educational and training policies in Latin America.

The same scheme of policy analysis considering education and training policies to complement the workings of market forces, together with policies combating imperfections and adverse institutional factors, can be applied to other kinds of skill differentials. A comprehensive set of policies would include not only those comparing broad catagories, like clerical, skilled, semi-skilled, and unskilled workers, but entering into finer occupational groups, like accountants, machinists, engineers, and foremen, where monopoly elements and natural abilities tend to require changes in the emphasis given to the various policies considered above.

Greater attention has been given in chapters 7 and 8, and in the appendix, to national policies relating to intracountry wage differentials. Emphasis has been placed in this concluding chapter only on the most important sources of labor income inequality in Latin America, including intracountry wage differentials due to varying skills. It seems appropriate to point out that the other differentials studied are also widespread in the area and require the attention of policy makers.

Appendix. Wage differentials in Mexico
by Adalberto García Rocha

In this appendix, the measurement of wage differentials is carried out using an information theory approach.[1] The method is then applied to a sample of firms in Mexico City. As the Mexican survey had less detailed information on workers' characteristics, the application of the methodology used in the other chapters of this book was not feasible.

Measurement of wage differentials using information theory

Two aspects of wage differentials will be considered: vertical occupational disparities basically due to differences in skills possessed by wage earners, and horizontal disparities due to differences among similar occupational categories (jobs or groups of jobs) in different economic units (firms, industries, etc.). To a considerable extent, differentials of the first type reflect the different contributions which employees make to production. Thus, the pay scale is supposedly related to skills, a proxy for intrinsic labor productivity. Within each firm, wages range from the low levels corresponding to unskilled manual workers, to the higher levels paid to technicians and administrative personnel. Ultimately, these differentials are substantially affected by relative scarcities of personnel and the interplay of market forces.

The horizontal differentials result from factors like differences in the cost of living in the areas where the industries or firms are established or in the relative importance assigned to different jobs in each industry or firm. For example, a chemist might not perform the same tasks in the chemical and food industries. Hence, his productivity may vary from one industry to the

NOTE: The author is a research economist at the Centro de Estudios Económicos y Demográficos of El Colegio de México. He thanks Pedro Uribe for valuable suggestions on the use of information theory in measuring differentials. He also wishes to acknowledge the most helpful comments made on various aspects of the chapter by Raúl de la Peña and Daniel Murayama of the Centro de Estudios Económicos y Demográficos of El Colegio de México. He is indebted to the computer centers of the Universidad Nacional Autónoma de México and Petróleos Mexicanos (PEMEX) for data processing and computation.

1. Pedro Uribe, "Concentración Demográfica y Estructura Urbana: un Enfoque via Teoría de la Información," *Demografía y Economía* 1, 1967, pp. 151–80.

other. These two kinds of wage differentials can be used as important guides in wage measurement.

If data on wage payments and employment classified by occupation and firm are available, we may define S_{ij} as payment for occupation i by firm j, and Q_{ij} as employment in occupation i and in firm j. Then, total payments would be $S = \sum_{ij} S_{ij}$ and total employment, $Q = \sum_{ij} Q_{ij}$, with the average salary equal to S/Q. Moreover, at the firm and occupational levels, payments and employment would be:

$$S_j = \sum_i S_{ij} \qquad\qquad Q_j = \sum_i Q_{ij}$$
$$S_i = \sum_j S_{ij} \qquad\qquad Q_i = \sum_j Q_{ij}.$$

Data on payments and manpower, thus defined, would allow an approximation of the discrete probability distributions:

$$\{w_{ij}\} = \left\{\frac{S_{ij}}{S}\right\}$$

and:

$$\{t_{ij}\} = \left\{\frac{Q_{ij}}{Q}\right\}.$$

The term w_{ij} is the relative proportion of wages for occupation i in firm j, and t_{ij} is the equivalent for employment.

Note that:

$$0 \leqslant w_{ij}, t_{ij} \leqslant 1$$

and that:

$$\sum_{ij} w_{ij} = \sum_{ij} t_{ij} = 1$$

Assume $w_{ij} = t_{ij}$ for all i and j, that is, for all firms and occupations. In this case, in all occupations and in all firms, wages are exactly alike and equal to the overall average wage. Any real life situation is far from a condition of equal wages, but this extreme case can be used as a model for comparing disparities. In other words, the extent to which w_{ij} differs from t_{ij} can be taken as the size of wage differentials. These differentials can be quantified in many ways, but in general any such index or measure should fulfill the following conditions:

(a) The index must be zero when $w_{ij} = t_{ij}$. This is the extreme case of no disparities.

(b) It must increase when the difference between w_{ij} and t_{ij} increases.

(c) The index should always be positive when w_{ij} and t_{ij} are not equal.

As an illustration, suppose that the proportion of typists in firm x is lower than the corresponding proportion of wages. This means that in other jobs and/or firms the opposite must hold true. The index will give identical figures if the situation is reversed, that is, if the proportion of typists in firm x is higher than the corresponding wages. However, if the index is broken down additively, it is possible to distinguish between the two cases.

Through the following identity, wage differentials can be measured:

$$I = \sum_{ij} W_{ij} \left(\log \frac{w_{ij}}{t_{ij}} \right) \text{ where } I \text{ is the index.} \qquad (1)$$

In information theory, this is termed indirect information with a priori probability t_{ij} and a posteriori probability w_{ij}.[2]

If $w_{ij} = t_{ij}$ for all i and j, identity (1) is transformed into:

$$I = \sum_{ij} w_{ij} (\log 1) = 0$$

which fulfills condition (a).

It has also been shown that:

$$\sum_{ij} w_{ij} \left(\log \frac{w_{ij}}{t_{ij}} \right) \geq \frac{1}{2} \sum_{ij} w_{ij} (w_{ij} - t_{ij})^2 \ \dagger$$

Letting the expression on the right equal any number, α, this inequality means that I is greater than zero if α is positive. This satisfies conditions (b) and (c).

It is useful to examine the structure of I using breakdowns which show the significant characteristics of the differentials described earlier. Such breakdowns can be made in various ways and the criteria for selecting any one of them will depend on its economic relevance.

First, it is necessary to make further definitions regarding the degree of aggregation of w_{ij} and t_{ij}. Occupations and firms can be aggregated to form occupational groups and industries respectively (see table A-1). Following a

2. F. Reza, *An Introduction to Information Theory* (New York: McGraw-Hill, 1961), pp. 104–5.

† C. Rao, *Linear Statistical Inference and its Applications* (New York: Wiley, 1967), p. 47.

Table A-1. Mexico: Aggregational forms of industries
and occupational groups

Occupational group	Occupation	Industry 1		Industry 2	
		Firm 1	Firm 2	Firm 1	Firm 2
Senior executives	Comptroller Manager	w_{11}	w_{12}	. . . .	
Middle executives	Purchasing chief Personnel chief	w_{11}	w_{12}	. . . .	
Manual workers	Bricklayer Oil worker Waiter Day laborer	w_{11}	w_{12}	. . . .	

design similar to the one in this table, $W_{ih} = \sum_{j\xi h} w_{ij}$ can be defined as the percentage of wages paid for occupation i in industry h made up by the firms $j\xi h$, where $j\xi h$ means firm j in industry h. Similarly $W_{gj} = \sum_{i\xi g} w_{ij}$ can be defined as the proportion of wages paid to the occupation group g by firm j.

The double aggregation, $W_{gh} = \sum_{i\xi g} \sum_{j\xi h} w_{ij}$, therefore represents payments to occupation group g by industry h. Partial aggregations, like W_{ih} and W_{gj}, as well as W_{gh}, exist for the t_{ij} distribution.

The aggregation in both directions is represented in table A-2, which shows G occupation groups and H industries. Horizontal and vertical totals of table A-2 are symbolized by:

$$W_G = \Sigma_h W_{gh} \text{ and } W_H = \Sigma_g W_{gh}.$$

Analysis of the differentials

If data were available only for wage payments and employment for occupation groups (i.e., if $\{W_g.\}$ and $\{T_g.\}$ were known), by analogy with (1) the index of salary differentials would be:

$$I = \sum_{g=1}^{G} W_g. \left(\log \frac{W_g.}{T_g.} \right) \qquad (2)$$

This measures the differentials between occupational groups without taking into account their distribution among industries and firms. If $\{W_g.\} = \{T_g.\}$ the mean salaries of each occupational group would be equal, although this does not imply that salaries would not vary among occupations within the group.

If data are available for occupation groups in different industries, it is

possible to measure those differentials within the group attributable to industrial differences. The conditional distribution $\{W_{gh} \mid W_g.\}$ refers to the internal industrial composition of group g; therefore, again by analogy with (1)
the corresponding differentials are:

$$\Sigma \frac{W_{gh}}{W_g.} \left(\log \frac{W_{gh}/W_g.}{T_{gh}/T_g.} \right) \tag{3}$$

After some algebraic manipulations, it can be shown that a measure of
wage differentials can be derived from expressions (2) and (3) which consid-
ers both variation over occupation groups and industries:

$$I = \sum_g \sum_h W_{gh} \left(\log \frac{W_{gh}}{T_{gh}} \right) \tag{4}$$

Of course, this assumes that the aggregate distributions $\{W_{gh}\}$ and $\{T_{gh}\}$
are known. Because of the way in which it was derived, (4) has two components: the differentials between occupation groups and the differentials
within groups attributable to industry differences. From this formula, the
combined differentials among industries and groups (the total differentials)
can be derived.

However, differentials exist within each industry-occupational group cell.
Take the information within each cell; if for industry 10, for example, the
percentages of wages and labor force corresponding to employees in occupation group 7 were known, it would be possible to measure the dispersion of

Table A-2. Mexico: Aggregation of occupational groups
and industries

Occupational group	Industry				
	1	2	. . . h	. . . H	
1	w_{11}	w_{12}	w_{1h}	w_{1H}	$W_1.$
2	w_{21}				$W_2.$
.					
.					
.					
g	w_{g1}				$W_g.$
.					
.					
.					
G	w_{G1}				$W_G.$
Total	$w_{.1}$			$W_{.H}$	

the occupations contained within cell (10,7). In general, if the composition of occupations in cell *(g,h)* is known, the following differential can also be calculated:

$$\sum_{i \xi G g} \frac{W_{ih}}{W_{gh}} \left(\log \frac{W_{ih}/W_{gh}}{T_{ih}/T_{gh}} \right) \tag{5}$$

In (5) a measurement of the wage differences among occupations within group *g* in industry *h* is obtained. To put it in another way, it measures differentials between occupations within cell *(g,h)*. The analog of this expression at the level of occupational groups is (2). From this follows the definition of the internal differential of occupation *(i)* within industry *(h)*, that is, between firms *(j):*

$$\sum_{j \xi Sh} \frac{w_{ij}}{W_{ih}} \left(\log \frac{w_{ij}/W_{ih}}{t_{ij}/T_{ih}} \right) \tag{6}$$

Summarizing, the wage differentials can be divided into two major groups, between cells and within cells. Differentials between cells consist of:

(i) Differentials among occupational groups.
(ii) Differentials among industries.

In turn, the within-cell differentials can be divided into:

(i) Differentials among occupations.
(ii) Differentials among firms.

This breakdown, given appropriate weights, is additive, giving a useful flexibility for interpreting the significance of each element of the differentials. By the same token, the relative importance of each element takes a clear economic meaning.

The differentials among firms in an industry and among industries are both horizontal. However, the first is defined in the context of this chapter as referring to a particular occupation, for example, variations in pay of electricians among the various firms in the chemical industry. On the other hand, the second kind is measured in terms of occupational groups, for example, differences in salaries paid to office personnel in different industries.

Differences among occupations in an occupation group and among occupation groups are both vertical. However, the differentials among occupations refer to particular firms, while those among occupation groups refer to a certain industry. An example of the first is the wage differential between janitors and electricians in a particular firm; an illustration of the second is the difference in pay between office workers and manual workers in a certain industry.

These types of wage differences measure the magnitude of the inducement to change occupation and place of employment, insofar as salaries are important in attracting or retaining manpower.

Application to the Mexican survey

In this section the information theory just discussed is applied to a sample of manufacturing firms within the Mexico City metropolitan area.[3] The information was gathered in December 1965 from approximately 92 firms and covered 97 different occupations, distributed as follows:

Occupation group	Occupations
1. Senior executives	7
2. Middle executives	19
3. Technical and professional personnel	12
4. Office personnel	29
5. Manual workers	30
Total	97

It included information on wages, fringe benefits, and the number of employees in each job. Therefore, this survey can be used to approximate the w_{ij} and t_{ij} distribution needed in the analysis of wage differentials using the information theory approach.

Hence, w_{ij} and t_{ij} comprised 97 jobs in 92 firms, covering these occupation groupings. These groups corresponded approximately to the concept of a job cluster defined as a grouping of jobs with similar characteristics regarding salary, role within the organization of the firm, technological levels, promotion policies, etc.[4]

The grouping of the firms into industries was limited by the amount of information available. As a result, it was necessary to work with highly aggregated industrial groups. Since industrial groups do not have a precise definition, their internal conformity cannot be guaranteed.[5] They are:

3. The author wishes to thank the Instituto de Participación de las Utilidades en el Salario, of the Confederación Patronal de la República Mexicana, for its generous assistance in the collection of the information on which this section of the study is based. See Instituto de Participación de las Utilidades en el Salário (IPAUS), Confederación Patronal de la Republica Mexicana (COPARMEX), *Encuesta Técnica sobre Salários y Prestaciones*, (Mexico Area Metropolitana, Mexico: D.F., 1966).

4. John T. Dunlop, "The Task of Contemporary Wage Theory" in *New Concepts in Wage Determination*, ed. George W. Taylor and Frank C. Pierson (New York: McGraw-Hill, 1957).

5. The wage survey in Mexico was in many ways broader than in the other countries as will be evident shortly. Among other things, the field work covered firms outside manufacturing. Although 150 firms were surveyed, not all were included in the study because poor data were obtained from some of them.

I. Food, beverage, tobacco, textiles, paper and paper products, printing, publishing and connected industries, rubber products.   17

II. Chemical products, non-metallic mineral products except for derivatives of petroleum and coal.   15

III. Basic metals, metal products, machinery and parts, electrical goods, transport material, construction, diverse manufacturing industries.   27

IV. Wholesale and retail commerce, insurance.   19

V. Mineral extraction, construction, water and related services, activities not clearly specified, storage and warehouse, public and personal services.   14

Total   92

Tables A-3 and A-4 present the distribution of employment and wages (w_{gh}) before and after taxes for the five occupation groups and the five industrial groupings just described.[6] Tables A-5 and A-6 show wages in relation to the overall wage average.

From table A-3 it can be seen that the last two occupational groups account for two-thirds of the total wage payments and 82.7% of the total employment. This gives an indication of the disproportionate distribution of wage payments between the first three and the last two groups.

Table A-5 shows that only the last occupational group (manual workers) has wages below the overall wage average. All other groups receive wages above the average. Table A-6 shows the influence of taxes on wages for the various groupings considered. It can be seen that the wage relatives of the lowest occupational group remain almost the same.

The distribution of wage payments by industrial groups is more uniform; three groups receive wages above the overall wage average, and two groups receive wages below it. The last industrial group, V, a catch-all category, appears to have the highest wages, and group III, metal industries, the lowest. These variations depend somewhat on the structure of the industry's employment. Note that in industry grouping III and IV middle rank executives have lower salaries when compared to those paid in other groups. Looking at senior executive salaries, those in group I are the best remunerated.

6. Income tax payments were calculated by applying the tax rates in effect during the year of the survey to the reported straight wages.

Table A-3. Mexico: Percentage distribution of employment and wage payments after taxes by occupational and industrial groups, December 1965[a]

Occupational group		Industrial group					Total
		I	II	III	IV	V	
1	Payments	2.02	1.74	2.42	1.80	0.90	8.93
	Employment	0.44	0.42	0.58	0.33	0.22	1.99
2	Payments	6.25	4.42	3.57	3.65	1.47	19.36
	Employment	3.18	1.84	2.24	1.92	0.73	9.91
3	Payments	1.94	1.53	1.66	1.90	0.53	6.56
	Employment	1.42	1.28	1.48	0.76	0.42	5.36
4	Payments	12.47	6.68	4.93	8.28	5.85	38.21
	Employment	10.15	6.53	6.86	9.68	4.18	37.40
5	Payments	8.61	5.18	9.78	2.12	1.24	26.93
	Employment	14.28	9.20	14.97	4.44	2.42	45.31
Total	Payments	31.29	19.55	22.41	16.75	9.99	100.00
	Employment	29.47	19.27	26.13	17.13	7.98	100.00

[a] See text for the identification of the occupational and industrial groups.

Table A-4. Mexico: Percentage distribution of employment and wage payments before taxes by occupational and industrial groups, December 1965[a]

Occupational group		Industrial group					Total
		I	II	III	IV	V	
1	Payments	2.14	1.84	2.62	1.95	0.95	9.50
	Employment	0.44	0.42	0.58	0.33	0.22	1.99
2	Payments	6.32	4.59	3.57	3.70	1.39	19.67
	Employment	3.18	1.84	2.24	1.92	0.73	9.91
3	Payments	1.94	1.52	1.64	0.88	0.52	6.50
	Employment	1.42	1.28	1.48	0.76	0.42	5.36
4	Payments	12.48	6.60	4.82	8.17	6.05	38.12
	Employment	10.15	6.53	6.86	9.68	4.19	37.41
5	Payments	8.38	5.04	9.52	2.05	1.20	26.19
	Employment	14.28	9.20	14.97	4.44	2.42	45.31
Total	Payments	31.26	19.50	22.17	16.75	10.21	100.00
	Employment	29.47	19.27	26.13	17.13	7.98	100.00

[a] See text for the identification of the occupational and industrial groups.

Table A-5. Mexico: Wages before taxes by occupational and industrial groups, relative to the overall average, December 1965[a]

Occupational group	Industrial group					All
	I	II	III	IV	V	
1	4.86	4.38	4.52	5.91	4.32	4.77
2	1.99	2.49	1.59	1.93	2.04	1.98
3	1.37	1.19	1.11	1.16	1.24	1.21
4	1.23	1.01	1.70	1.84	1.44	1.02
5	0.59	0.55	0.64	0.46	0.50	0.58
All	1.06	1.02	0.85	0.98	1.28	-

[a]See text for the identification of the occupational and industrial groups.

Table A-6. Mexico: Wages after taxes by occupational and industrial groups, relative to the overall average, December 1965[a]

Occupational group	Industrial group					All
	I	II	III	IV	V	
1	4.49	4.14	4.26	5.45	4.09	4.49
2	1.96	2.40	1.59	1.90	2.01	1.95
3	1.37	1.20	1.12	1.18	1.26	1.22
4	1.23	1.02	0.72	0.86	1.40	1.02
5	0.60	0.56	0.65	0.48	0.51	0.59
All	1.06	1.01	0.86	0.98	1.25	-

[a]See text for the identification of the occupational and industrial groups.

With regard to wage payments by occupational groups, there is a striking difference between the salaries of senior executives and the wages of all the other categories. The rankings conform exactly to the ordering given to the occupational groups, forming a vertical wage scale which is not changed by taxation.

The overall differences in table A-7 and A-8 show, as might be expected, that vertical wage differences (those among occupations and occupational groups) are much greater than horizontal differences (those among firms and industries). In fact, about 75% of the total wage disparities are vertical and only about 25% horizontal. This means that salary changes are much greater when an employee moves up the wage scale than when he remains in the same occupation but moves to another firm or industry. The differences among occupation groups are largest which indicates that the best chance for a substantial salary increase results from a change in occupational group rather than changing occupations within the same grouping, or shifting to another firm or industry.

The three highest groups have greater possibilities for improving labor income through occupational mobility than the two lower groups. For office workers and manual workers to move into any of the other three groups, and particularly into technical and professional personnel, requires a substantial improvement in educational level. There are fewer problems of this kind involved in changes among the three higher groups. Hence, possibilities of improvement in the last two groups are mostly limited to either intragroup changes in occupation or horizontal mobility.

Although overall differentials diminish when taxes are taken into account, the structure changes only slightly with vertical or scale differentials becoming more prominent in relative terms (see tables A-7 and A-8). Due to the nature of the tax laws, the differentials among wages in the same income bracket are reduced more than the differentials in wages in different brackets.

Table A-7. Mexico: Differentials in wages before taxes among and within occupations and occupational groups, December 1965[a]

Category	Among		Within		Total	
	Absolute	%	Absolute	%	Absolute	%
Occupations	0.1171	31.6	0.0791	21.3	0.1962	52.9
Occupational groups	0.1601	43.1	0.0148	4.0	0.1749	47.1
Total	0.2772	74.7	0.0939	25.3	0.3711	100.0

[a] Differences within occupations are horizontal differentials among firms while those within occupational groups are horizontal inter-industrial differentials. Those existing among occupations and occupational groups are vertical differentials.

Table A-8. Mexico: Differentials in wages after taxes among and within occupations and occupational groups, December 1965[a]

Category	Among		Within		Total	
	Absolute	%	Absolute	%	Absolute	%
Occupations	0.1082	32.2	0.0695	20.7	0.1175	52.9
Occupational groups	0.1449	43.2	0.0130	3.9	0.1579	47.1
Total	0.2529	75.4	0.0825	24.6	0.3354	100.0

[a] Differences within occupations are horizontal differentials among firms while those within occupational groups are horizontal inter-industrial differentials. Those existing among occupations and occupational groups are vertical differentials.

Thus, horizontal differentials, which are smaller and tend to occur within the income brackets, lose some of their relative importance after taxes are taken into account. This last observation raises interesting points about the characteristics of the tax system, and could offer a criterion for modifying tax policy in order to secure greater redistribution of wage income across occupations and occupation groups.

Some of these differentials can be broken down even further by looking into some of the broader classifications. Table A-9, for example, presents such a breakdown for occupation groups both before and after taxes, showing the wage differentials inside each of the groups. For the same occupation group, differentials among occupations and among firms are presented. Office personnel shows the widest disparities overall. When office personnel and manual workers are grouped together they account for the larger part of

Table A-9. Mexico: Wage differentials among and within occupational groups, December 1965[a]

Before taxes				
Occupational group	Interoccupation		Interfirm	
	Absolute	Percent	Absolute	Percent
Senior executives	0.0033	3.8	0.0072	9.1
Middle executives	0.0163	13.9	0.0170	21.5
Technical and professional personnel	0.0026	2.2	0.0033	4.2
Office personnel	0.659	56.3	0.0448	56.6
Manual workers	0.0290	24.8	0.0068	8.6
Total	0.1171	100.0	0.0791	100.0

After taxes				
Occupational group	Interoccupation		Interfirm	
	Absolute	Percent	Absolute	Percent
Senior executives	0.0027	2.5	0.0060	8.6
Middle executives	0.0142	13.2	0.0147	21.1
Technical and professional personnel	0.0024	2.2	0.0031	4.4
Office personnel	0.0604	56.0	0.0390	56.2
Manual workers	0.0282	26.1	0.0067	9.7
Total	0.1079	100.0	0.0695	100.0

[a]See note to table A-7.

the wage differentials: 81% of the total interoccupational variation and 65% of the interfirm variation.

This concentration of differentials in two groups may be due to wide or otherwise inadequate occupational groupings. However, the relative importance of interfirm wage differentials in the office personnel category suggests that, assuming similar skills, certain variables at the firm level also have an important influence on total wage dispersion in this group. In addition, in this occupational group the most marked differences occur between starting wages and average wages, even though office workers probably have the most common and best specified jobs. After what has been said, it would appear that the much wider differentials in the wages of office workers could not be attributed to greater heterogeneity of occupations within the group. In the case of manual workers, the wide dissimilarities are probably due to influences of labor unions, as well as to a considerable heterogeneity in their functions.

In the first three groups, differentials corresponding to middle executives are the largest. Only one fifth of the total wage variation is explained by interoccupational variation, while almost a third corresponds to interfirm variation. The large part played by firm differentials, particularly in the second occupational group, may result from the shortage of qualified personnel and low mobility in these groupings. In the case of middle management, the wider interfirm differentials might reflect relatively "firm-specific" skills. It should be noted that the technical and professional group, which consists more of technicians rather than administrative personnel, shows very low wage variation.

Taxes accentuate the differentials of the manual workers' group in both categories, as well as the interfirm differentials of the technical and professional group in relative terms (see last two columns of table A-9). This is mostly because taxes are less steep in the lower brackets.

Comparison with previous results

In the main part of this book, wage differentials have been studied separately for each occupation or position, the objective having been to ascertain the influence of job content (as reflected in education, experience, and degree of responsibility), size of firm, industry, and country. Those results brought out the manner in which these variables influence wages in these particular occupations. A somewhat different point of view has been taken in this appendix, namely, to investigate the relative importance of the differences *among* occupations and *among* industries, when all occupations and industries are combined. Moreover, occupational differences have been segmented into differences among occupational groups and into differences within occupational groups in terms of variation among positions within each of the five occupation groups outlined at the beginning of section A.2.

The principal results, in tables A-7 through A-9, indicate that by far the most important source of wage differentials in this context are the differences among occupational groups, a finding that holds whether these differentials are computed before or after taxes. At the same time, variations among occupations within the same occupation group are also quite important, especially for office personnel and manual workers. From an overall point of view, wage differentials in the same occupation groups among different industries are of relatively minor consequence, though these interindustry differentials are somewhat more important for individual occupations within these broader occupational groups.

These results serve to reinforce the rationale underlying the job cluster approach taken in the preceding chapters, by highlighting the importance of occupational differences as distinct from industry differences in explaining wage differentials. In other words, this appendix has shown that the differentials among occupations, at least in Mexico in the industries studied, are very substantial and require separate study, which is what has been done in this book.

Index

171